# Earth
# Day
# Reconsidered

Edited by
## JOHN BADEN

## The Heritage Foundation
*Washington, D.C.*

The preparation of this manuscript is being supported by The Heritage Foundation. The manuscript is based substantially on material and ideas generated at a conference that was organized and directed cooperatively by the Liberty Fund and the Center for Political Economy and Natural Resources, and held in Gallatin County, Montana, in September of 1978.

John Baden is an environmentalist, political economist, and sometimes a logger. He is the co-author (with Garrett Hardin) of *Managing The Commons*, and author of many articles in the field of natural resources policy. Dr. Baden currently is Director of the Center for Political Economy and Natural Resources at Montana State University.

---

Library of Congress Catalog card number 80-81670

ISBN 0-89195-028-1

# Table of Contents

## PART ONE

**Chapter 1**
Introduction—Ubiquity & Reality: The Environment and Self-
Interest                                                                        1
*John Baden*

**Chapter 2**
Good Intentions and Self-Interest: Lessons from the American
Indian                                                                           5
*John Baden, Richard L. Stroup* and *Wally Thurman*

**Chapter 3**
Environmentalists and Self-Interest: How Pure are Those Who
Desire the Pristine?                                                            13
*John Baden, Randy Simmons,* and *Rodney D. Fort*

## PART TWO

**Chapter 4**
Environmental Quality, Social Welfare, and Bureaucratic
Pathologies                                                                     33
*John Baden* and *Richard L. Stroup*

**Chapter 5**
Compounding Clearcuts: The Social Failures of Public Timber
Management in the Rockies                                                       43
*William F. Hyde* as adapted by *Kay Blemker*

**Chapter 6**
An Institutional Dinosaur with an Ace: or, How to Piddle Away
Public Timber Wealth and Foul the Environment in the Process    49
*Barney Dowdle* as adapted by *Kay Blemker*

**Chapter 7**
Dams and Other Disasters: The Social Costs of Federal Water
Development Policies                                                    55
*Bernard Shanks* as adapted by *Kay Blemker*

**Chapter 8**
Policy-Induced Demand for Coal Gasification                            63
*Richard L. Stroup* as adapted by *Kay Blemker*

## PART THREE

**Chapter 9**
Property Rights, Cowboys and Bureaucrats: A Modest Proposal    71
*John Baden*

**Chapter 10**
Property Rights and Natural Resources: Applications                    83
*John Baden* and *Richard L. Stroup*

**Chapter 11**
The Federal Budget as a Common Pool Resource: the Develop-
ment of a Predatory Bureaucracy                                        95
*John Baden* and *Rodney D. Fort*

**Chapter 12**
Concluding Thoughts                                                   105
*M. Bruce Johnson*

# Acknowledgements:

# Earth Day Reconsidered

This volume has emerged as a natural and indeed almost accidental product of a Liberty Fund conference organized by the Center for Political Economy and Natural Resources and of my fifteen years as an environmental activist. Perhaps because of my farm background, I developed more sensitivity to natural resource and environmental matters than to other "social problems." On Earth Day 1970 I discovered that my concerns were shared by millions of Americans. I have since learned that deep concern and good intention are insufficient. A basic understanding of the incentives contained within a program of improvement is requisite to systematic success. It is my hope that this volume will add to a general understanding of processes that can lead to high quality resource management.

I did not enter the Environmental Decade of the '70's with all of the right answers. I have, however, had several excellent teachers as I worked through the decade and I owe them my thanks. They include Del Gardner, Garrett Hardin, Vince Ostrom, and Rick Stroup. It is gratifying to receive intellectual and moral support from individuals such as these. It is also gratifying to have the promise of one's work recognized by foundations. This volume, and other work from the Center for Political Economy and Natural Resources, has been supported by AMAX, The Heritage Foundation, The Liberty Fund, and The Scaife Family Charitable Trust. The support of these organizations plus the encouragement and support of Montana State University and numerous individuals fosters the dissemination of our analysis and perspective. On behalf of the Center I express my thanks for all who have contributed to this effort.

John Baden

# Part One

# 1

## Introduction—
## Ubiquity and Reality:
## The Environment and Self-Interest

Earth Day, April 22, 1970, gave great impetus to the environmental movement. It fostered what I consider a highly favorable reorientation toward the American environment. Until the Spring of 1970, concern with natural resource and environmental policy was primarily restricted to a few economists, a much smaller number of political scientists, sociologists and other social and natural scientists, and several established interest groups. Although attention to the issues of human-ecosystem interaction had shown substantial growth in the 1960's, there was an explosion of interest associated with Earth Day in April of 1970.[1] With this event, ecology, formerly a somewhat esoteric branch of biology, gained currency and wide recognition. This concern with environmental quality and resource management clearly had the potential for fostering considerable improvements in net social welfare. Yet, the potential has not been recognized. I am an environmentalist with a deep concern for individual freedom and for the efficient utilization of resources. I view the tenth anniversary of Earth Day as an opportunity to reconsider several of the fundamental issues inherently associated with the environmental movement.

A review of the decade indicates that Americans in general came to realize that there are tradeoffs associated with our traditional pattern of growth and development. A substantial proportion decided, at least in principle, that the costs of growth often swamp the benefits. The social costs of pollution, clearcutting, and population growth were increasingly recognized, and the term "externalities" appeared in the popular press and served as verbal fodder at cocktail parties. With a few exceptions, such as Boulding, economists tended to be viewed as

---

[1] One book, one of the many generated by this new market, was entitled, *Earth Day: The Beginning....*

1

defenders of an obsolete and dysfunctional order while the social stock of biologists clearly increased. Concurrently, colleges and universities established multi-disciplinary programs in environmental studies while enrollments in the traditional natural resource fields of forestry and wildlife increased dramatically. Further, public opinion polls indicated that environmental issues displaced other policy concerns as critical issues. In sum, environmentalism became a genuine social movement.

Although the natural environment is indeed competitive, to the participants it may seem Edenesque when compared with the elective arena. Thus political entrepreneurs discovered a new niche to exploit. The defeat of Wayne Aspinal and the election of Dick Lamm in Colorado were both attributable to a changing political environment. It is useful to view politics as the process that formulates rules for economic activity. While politics are also a recreational and (for some) a religious exercise, the dominant impact of politics is economic. Politics influence how resources are allocated. Politics skew opportunities. For one concerned with welfare, politics matter. Obviously.

Those active in a democratic political process normally require an ideological basis to justify proposed changes in the rules of the game. If a coherent ideology is unavailable or if the information costs of educating people to that ideology are very high, then a few relatively simple statements will often suffice. The following is a brief and incomplete catalogue of such statements. Each has the advantage of being substantiated by at least casual observation. Each also has the advantage of offering the politician an opportunity for bamboozle, i.e., for hiding or diffusing costs and concentrating and advertising benefits.

1) The claim was that Americans, especially other Americans, are excessively and rashly materialistic, egocentric, and self-interested. This is perhaps most evident in their choice of transportation, i.e., the personal car, which is consumptive of both resources and degrading of environmental quality.

2) American business is mesmerized by profits and is perfectly willing to sacrifice environmental health for corporate wealth. This is epitomized by the production of noxious smoke, dangerous chemicals, and externalities in general.

3) Americans stress property rights in a manner which diminishes social welfare. Thus, the reasoning goes, if more management and control are given to the public sector bureaucrats who can realize no profits, then the public interest will be fostered. Under these circumstances individuals will lack the incentive to sacrifice public welfare for personal gain.

2

While the above considerations are not exhaustive, I trust they are at least illustrative of the ideas and the ideology which developed with the environmental movement. This orientation represents a fundamental challenge to the ideological foundations of the American experiment. It is clear that the policies adopted in response to the environmental movement have produced substantial benefits. It is also obvious that they have generated costs, transferred wealth, and reduced efficiencies. On the tenth anniversary of Earth Day, it is time for a re-evaluation. The fundamental goal of advancing welfare by acknowledging the value of environmental goods can easily accept a reasoned challenge. Yet, the means often adopted to obtain this goal are basically flawed. In brief, we have adopted extremely expensive mechanisms to buy increments in environmental quality. The relative contributions of altruism and self-interest incentives have been misunderstood and hence incorrectly evaluated. A reassessment is in order. This book represents a preliminary step in the direction of our efforts to obtain higher measures of environmental quality and to do so at a lower price in terms of efficiency and freedom sacrificed.

This book is one of advocacy. It advocates environmental quality, economic efficiency, and it especially advocates individual freedom. Further, it recognizes the necessity of tradeoffs among these values. While we cannot maximize all values concurrently, we can substantially improve upon our current attainments. Unless we are willing to rely upon luck, a basic understanding of the system is the prime requisite. Let us begin.

# 2

## Good Intentions and Self-Interest: Lessons From the American Indian

### Introduction

A decade ago many environmentalists believed that the proper combination of good intentions and competent bureaucrats would solve or ameliorate any problem of resource policy. Although our public resource managers tend to have both of these attributes, our experience suggests that a prudent person will not count on this conjunction as sufficient for the task. We first address the issue of "good intentions."

There are two myths in the American political system whose implications are socially expensive to hold. One is that fundamental problems can be solved by appointing the "right" people. This may be construed to mean that incentives do not matter and that the characteristics of individuals in office are controlling. This myth should be recognized but its exposure must wait until section two. The second myth, the one addressed in this chapter, is that culture can "rewire" people in such a manner that the public interest *becomes* self-interest. Alternatively, self-interest can be eliminated. While such a belief may appeal to some people's noble preferences, we believe that it is expensive in terms of success if people rely on such a belief. This chapter explores an alternative approach to gaining cooperation for attaining social goals. This alternative is based upon assumptions of basic principles of human behavior. These are:

1) People choose purposefully, tending to pick the options they expect to benefit from the most.

2) People respond to relative "prices." If an action is made more costly, it will be taken less frequently; if rewarded more, it will be taken more frequently. Incentives matter.

This is adapted from "Myths, Admonitions and Rationality: The American Indian as a Resource Manager" by John Baden, Richard Stroup, and Wally Thurman, forthcoming in *Economic Inquiry*.

3) Information is scarce and costly so that ignorance is often rational, especially when a decision will not be controlled by the individual. Uncertainty is a fact of life.

4) An economic system, like an ecologic system, is strongly interconnected; a policy action may have its intended effects but will probably have unintended side effects.

5) There is no free lunch. Collective decisions and governmental provision of goods can break the link between an individual's consumption and his payment, but then others must pay.

6) Exchange is *not* a zero sum game. Even without added production, *everyone* can be made better off. Higher profits, for example, *can* be accompanied by increased consumer well being.

We share these ideas with many political economists and others doing policy-relevant scholarly work. The principles are invaluable in our work and in theirs, providing much insight into how policy systems work, and why they often do not. These principles provide analytical leverage. They are empirical statements and are subject to potential disconfirmation. With a focus upon numbers one and two, let us examine some cross cultural data.

First we ask the following: is there in our historical experience a set of cultures in which self-interest is ideally subservient to living in ecological harmony? If such cultures have existed, do the cultural norms control or do the people behave as our assumptions suggest they will?

Social scientists have long argued over the role played by cultural norms in the determination of a people's behavior. The simultaneous development of a society's ideals of behavior and its observed behavior patterns generates much confusion in such discussions. Does the causal relationship run from culture to behavior or from behavior to culture? The question has proven to be incredibly complex and not very amenable to scientific resolution. A particular instance where the controversy has been played out in detail concerns the relationship between primitive people's environmental attitudes and their behavior towards the natural environment.

As political economists we are tempted to bypass the strict question of causality and to apply the paradigm of microeconomics in a predictive sense. The question then becomes: can economic theory successfully predict primitive people's environmental behavior from observable phenomena? By phrasing the question this way we hope to explain such behavior without relying on the black box of culture.

In particular, this paper tests the applicability of microeconomics to

6

data from the American Indian cultures. After a review of historical evidence the policy implications for current environmental problems are discussed.

## American Indians and Environmentally Optimal Behavior

The most outstanding features of the North American Indian groupings were the great variations evidenced in their cultures. They ranged from the simplest hunting-gathering bands to empires, from the extreme poverty of the Great Basin to the affluence of the Northwest Coast. Yet it is generally held that these highly diverse groups shared a common reverence for the land and the interdependencies of nature that provided man his niche. This point is well defined in several papers and there is no need to add to the evidence here. The implications of this view are perhaps most explicitly expressed by Vine Deloria, who stated that the white man "...must quickly adopt not just the contemporary Indian world view but the ancient Indian world view to survive."[1]

The actual behavior attributed to these cultures reads like an admonition from Francis of Assisi, the patron saint of the ecology movement. The native Americans are believed to have been non-materialistic and not guilty of conspicuous consumption. Consumption was geared to what was actually needed rather than to impressing the White Fox Lodge or the Bear Who Stands Up family. In general, rather than being influenced by price, measures of present value, or the decisions of bureaucratic managers of resources, behavior was guided by cultural traditions that incorporated generations of ecological understanding.

The very high degree of incorporation of nature into the native religions was found throughout all regions of North America. The material offered by Steffansson on the Eskimo, Lowie on the Crow, and Spicer on the Southwest tribes strongly supports this statement.

This same appreciation extended to the utilitarian. The beneficial and non-wasteful use that man made of nature is reflected in the fact that among the Blackfoot alone over 100 different uses were found for one animal, the buffalo. To some, this record makes the behavior of today's sport hunter obscene.

On the basis of the material presented above it appears evident that the Indian culture is highly consistent with the requirements of spaceship earth. One may be strongly tempted to go further and agree with Deloria that the adoption of Indian values is a requisite to successful accommodation of man to his environment. The conclusion that good

---

[1] *We Talk, You Listen*, MacMillan Co., 1970, p. 195.

values are necessary for good behavior is not of much help, however, in bringing about the desired outcome. The conservationist who puts all his faith in the alteration of value systems finds himself with little policy leverage. The scientist who relies upon value shifts to explain behavioral changes finds himself with models of little predictive power. The question we explore is: how far can one go in explaining environmental behavior without appealing to differences or changes in environmental values?

Economic theory assumes that people everywhere respond to relative prices or, in other words, to real opportunity costs. The economics texts don't say Americans, or Swedes, or Eskimos, or Arabs—they say people. Most simply, the law of demand states that the more a person has to give up to obtain a good, the less of that good is demanded. The principle of diminishing marginal utility states that the more of a good a person has, the less he will give up for an additional unit. In application, we would expect that while the contemporary American may be willing to sacrifice to protect highly valued endangered species, one would not expect a similar sacrifice to be made for a wild animal which is commonplace.

If these laws are correct and general, they apply to Indians. Let us then test for correctness and generality by examining the behavior of Indians to see if it is consistent with the above laws.

Theory postulates that Indians, regardless of their culture, will behave toward environmental goods (natural resources) like any other people. In general, when the cost to users of these goods is high, little will be demanded; and, when the cost is low, more will be demanded. To put this theory to the test we examine both cross sectional and time series observations.

## Property Rights and the Plains Indian Culture

The Indians of the American Plains are among the most well known and eulogized of all tribal peoples. The culture for which they are famous was of only short duration and was based on the horse and the buffalo.

Prior to the introduction of the horse, the hunting of bison was uncertain, and relatively unproductive. In the pre-horse period the capture of a buffalo was comparatively rare. Its biomass was highly valued and hence fully utilized.

In effect, the introduction of the horse, steel tools and later firearms lowered the "price" of the animal. As the price fell due to technological adaptation, patterns of utilization changed dramatically. During this period many buffalo were killed by Indians merely for the tongue and the two strips of back strap. By 1840 the Indian had driven the buffalo from portions of its original habitat. There is evidence of concern about this occurrence. Earl F. Murphy states that "[O]nly the simplicity of weaponry and the small number of these nomadic peoples kept the buffalo from meeting its fate two centuries earlier."[2] Compounding this shift in technology was the Indian's new access to the white man's market for hides. Thus, there was both a supply shift from lower costs of production and a new use of buffalo (sales) which effected an increase in demand.

Thus, in observing the Plains Indians we witness *efficient* behavioral adjustment to changing prices but *inefficient* management of a common property resource. Given multiple tribes, a fugitive resource, and high transaction costs, the Indians were incapable of establishing property rights and managing the buffalo as a renewable resource. Regardless of the ideology of the resource users, it is obvious that wise use is difficult to achieve when property rights are undefined and unenforced. When resources are communally owned, i.e., where private property rights are not established, ecologically damaging behavior is fostered. In this case the benefits from harvesting additional buffalo accrued to the individual hunter and his group while the costs of depletion of the herd were distributed among all potential hunters. In such a common property context, the full costs of hunting are not borne by the hunter and over-use is predictable.

### Property Rights and Institutional Adaptations: The Coastal Fur Trade

One of the first systematic explications of the development of property rights is Demsetz's treatment of the fur trade in North America.[3] The institution of private hunting territories among the Labrador Peninsula (Montagnais) Indians was described by the anthropologist, Frank Speck.[4]

The Montagnais Indians were primarily hunters subsisting on large game such as caribou and small fur-bearers such as beaver. Prior to the development of trade with Europeans there was little pressure upon

[2] Murphy, E. F., *Governing Nature*, Quadrangle Press, 1967, p. 99.
[3] See the writings of Eleanor Leacock, John M. Cooper, Loren C. Eiseley, and A. Irving Hallowell. Probably the first to subject the Montagnais to economic analysis was Harold Demsetz in the article "Toward a Theory of Property Rights," *American Economic Review*, May 1967, 57, pp. 347–73.
[4] Speck, Frank G., "A Report on Tribal Boundaries and Hunting Areas of the Malecite Indians of New Brunswick," *American Anthropologist*, 48:361 (1946).

these resources. Demand was below carrying capacity and the tribes hunted communally, sharing the harvest. With the establishment of the French fur trade routes in the early 1600's came the incentive for over-exploitation of the resource. With the beaver increasing in value, scarcity, depletion and localized extinction could be predicted under the existing system of property rights. But unlike the buffalo, virtually condemned to extinction as common property, the beaver were protected by the evolution of private property rights among their hunters. By the early to mid-18th century, the transition to private hunting grounds was almost complete and the Montagnais were managing the beaver on a sustained yield basis. Eleanor Leacock notes that trappers readily adopted conservation practices when they were able to personally collect the benefits. She notes[5] that, "[t]he Western Montagnais farms his territory by marking his houses, ascertaining the number of beavers in them, and always leaving at least a pair." The system of private ownership developed parallel to the fur trade. Leacock[6] observed "an unmistakable correlation between early center of trade and the oldest and most complete development of the hunting territory."

The difference in behavior between the beaver and the buffalo hunters may be traced to the different institutional structures. The inherent characteristics of the resources are fundamentally different, i.e., while the buffalo is a fugitive resource, beaver are sedentary and thus are amenable to private appropriations. Further, the transaction costs for a relatively homogeneous group of tribes such as the Montagnais are lower than among the warring Plains tribes. Thus, institutional accommodation should be easier to achieve.

With the significant intrusion of the white trapper in the 19th century, the Indian's property rights were violated. Because the Indian could not exclude the white trapper from the benefits of conservation both joined in trapping out the beaver.

A similar shift to the mining of beaver by the Algonquin relatives of the Montagnais, the Malecite, is described by Speck.[7]

> The occasion for this change in Indian sentiment regarding conservation was made plain by the informant's declarations that the native hunters, seeing that the whites were bent on wholesale destruction of the game

---

[5]Leacock, Eleanor, "The Montagnais 'Hunting Territory' and the Fur Trade," *American Anthropologist* vol. 56, no. 5, part 2, memoir no. 78, (1954) p. 35.

[6]Leacock, p. 12.

[7]See Heizer, R. F., "Primitive Man as an Ecologic Factor," *Kroeber Anthropological Society Papers No. 15.* Univ. of California Press, 1955; also, Speck, Frank G., "Land Ownership Among Hunting Peoples in Primitive America and the World's Marginal Areas," *Twenty-second International Congress of Americanists*, vol. 2, p. 323.

animals and fur-bearers, deliberately decided to take their share and profits from the forests before it became too late, and did so. And thus the epoch of conservative, regulated hunting by the Malecite...came quite abruptly to an end.

In essence, the Indians lost their ability to enforce property rights and rationally stopped practicing resource conservation.

## Culture and Environmental Quality

The claim that an environmentally sensitive culture, a culture in which self-interest is made subservient to environmental quality, is a sufficient condition for environmentally sensitive behavior is inconsistent with data from North American Indian cultures. Can we conclude from this evidence that culture has nothing to do with behavior relevant to the natural environment? Is the "land ethic" advocated by Aldo Leopold[8] to be dismissed as uninfluential on the matrix of man-nature relations?

Clearly, there is a relationship among beliefs, values, and man's treatment of his environment. It is not, however, as simple as stating: environmentally sensitive culture leads to environmentally sensitive behavior.

The overwhelming majority of the environmental problems faced by any society result from the logic of the commons. The potential for solving a common pool problem is largely dependent on the physical details of the individual resource. But unless the institutions of the society operate to protect the commons as the Montagnais protected their beaver resource, there are rewards which favor those who fail to practice conservation.

It is clear that if there is a cultural change such that people appreciate, respect, understand, and value environmental systems to a higher degree than is now the case, greater pressure will be placed on policy makers to protect our common pool resources. This pressure will result in legal and institutional modifications that produce a different pattern of information and incentives. Since it appears that people do respond as predicted by economic theory, these incentives will lead people to modify their behavior. If properly designed, these institutions and laws will encourage behavior that is rational at both the individual and the social level.

It is to the establishment of these policies and institutions that we

---

[8] Leopold, Aldo, *A Sand County Almanac and Sketches From Here and There*, Oxford University Press 1949.

should direct our attention if we are concerned with fostering environmental quality and efficient resource utilization while guarding individual freedom.

Although an environmentally sensitive culture cannot guarantee environmentally sensitive behavior by decision makers, it surely can aid in the establishment of the appropriate institutions.

The fundamental point of this chapter is: if the goal is to achieve improvements in environmental quality, good intentions will not suffice. Thus we should not rely solely upon good intentions toward Mother Earth. Rather, like the Indians of the Labrador Peninsula, we should focus our efforts upon institutional design with a particular emphasis upon property rights. Resources in common ownership offer extremely perverse incentives that foster over-exploitation, inefficiencies, and social conflict. Given the consistently demonstrated behavior of people, we should accept that self-interest exists and design our institutions accordingly.

# 3

## Environmentalists and Self-Interest:
## How Pure Are Those Who Desire the Pristine?

Some environmental and natural resource policy conflicts are discussed in terms of good versus bad, of those representing the public interest against those with the selfish goals of self-interest and profits. From the perspective of some environmentalists, self-interest is inherently evil while profit, rather than a reward for moving resources to more highly valued uses, should be a four letter word. Discussions of timber harvest often follow this format. The forest products industry is viewed either as a rapacious despoiler of pristine environments or the introducer of monocultures to formerly complex systems rather than being viewed as the supplier of valued products for citizens. We are both.[1]

On this matter there are two assertions whose validity is generally accepted. First, from the standpoint of social welfare the timber inventory of the United States was excessive in 1880. In other words, the social value of forest land and its endowment is higher in uses other than primeval forest. Second, people place a positive value on both forests and forest products. Even those who derive no pleasure from forests derive utility from its marketed products.

In marked contrast to the above group are those who derive aesthetic or recreational utility from forests. Such individuals often consider themselves and their allies self-sacrificing defenders of the public interest. Since they are not motivated by profit, we are to assume that their motives are pure. From our perspective however, the case is not so clear.

While some in the forest products industry may sincerely believe that theirs is the sacred mission to bring housing to the poor, most would probably agree that theirs is primarily a business that must confront

John Baden with Randy Simmons and Rodney Fort
[1]Having been a logger and a timber buyer I stand accused. Whether I feel that the accusation has merit or feel guilty is quite another matter.

the reality checks of budget sheets. Surely the survivors in this competitive industry would tend to fall in the latter category. In contrast, a
substantial proportion of those who use the political process to restrict
forests to recreation do so in the belief that theirs is a just, or even a
holy, cause. If the population were comprised of Druids they would be
correct. From the perspective of the recreationists the important point
is that self-interest is monopolized by the other side. In this chapter an
alternative view is presented. The situation is one in which the political
process is utilized to allocate resources. While the cardinal rule of economics is that there is no free lunch, that of politics is that others can
be made to pay. This may be one such case.

**Recreation and the Forest Commons**

It is generally recognized that the resources in a "commons" tend to
be utilized in a socially non-optimal manner. The large volume of literature dealing with common pool resources consistently shows over-
exploitation resulting from a divergence of private and social costs. In
brief, when costs are socialized and benefits are privatized, over-pro-
duction results. It is normally assumed that the resulting over-produc-
tion impoverishes environmental quality. This outcome, however, can
be quite different when the resource being produced is a set of environmental amenities. The logic remains intact but the outcome is non-
intuitive.

Most of the lakes, streams, mountain ranges, and forests in the
United States are held in common by the American people. There are
no strictly defined or enforced private property rights and spillover effects—higher wood prices and unemployment—are prevalent results of
individual actions within this commons setting. The key to this di-
lemma of common property is that the costs associated with the actions
of any single user of the commons are dispersed among the entire community while that individual captures all of the benefits. When the utilization of a commons generates individual benefits while costs are
shared by all users, the individual's share of the costs is only a fraction
of unity. Thus, the incentive for any individual is to continually increase personal use of the resource until his incremental costs equal his
incremental benefits. When all users pursue such a course the result is
often tragic and always, as in the case currently under consideration,
detrimental to the socially optimum utilization of the resources.
Typically, the commons is pushed beyond future productivity. The outputs of common pool resources are over-produced at a socially non-
optimal rate.

## The American Forests: Creation of a Regulated Commons

America's forest lands provide one example of a common resource. Early colonizers were blessed and damned with seemingly endless tracts of mature forests. The presence of excess inventory fostered the cutting of mature timber with essentially no thought given to regeneration. This was an inventory adjustment process. Wood was abundant and more land was desired for agricultural purposes. The marginal social value of food crops was higher than the marginal social value of timber. The process of inventory adjustment carried out the trade-off between agricultural and forest lands. In the absence of well defined and enforced property rights the motto of the age seemed to be "cut out and get out." This philosophy may have been both socially and privately optimal depending upon the relative value of standing mature timber and the value of alternative uses of former forest lands.

Public pressure mounted in the late 1800's to halt the generally perceived unbridled exploitation of the forests. This attitude indicates an awareness of the increasing potential scarcity and over-exploitation resulting from treatment of the forests as a commons. Decreasing inventories raised the expected future value of the forests and paved the way for the politically enforced consideration of the future. Congress authorized withdrawal of the forest reserves from the public domain in 1891. The Bureau of Forestry, renamed the Forest Service in 1905, was directed to manage the national forests "for the greatest good to the largest number of people in the long run." In effect, a commons of more restricted entry was created but the logic of common resource use remains intact.

## The New Wave: The Outdoor Recreation Deluge

Until the mid-1950's, recreational use of the national forests was limited to a slowly increasing group of outdoor enthusiasts. Since that time the increased mobility, leisure time, and spending power of Americans has led many more people into the woods seeking recreational and aesthetic amenities. Figure 1 indicates the rapid increase in the total number of recreational visits to all sites. R. W. Behan characterized the invasion, for a literal invasion it was, as the Outdoor Recreation Deluge (henceforth denoted ORD).[2] The public flooded the woods with camping trailers, snowmobiles, canoes, kayaks, and cross-country skis. To participants in the ORD, recreational and aesthetic amenities increased

---

[2]See R. W. Behan, "The Myth of the Omnipotent Forester," *Journal of Forestry*. Vol. 64, No. 6 (1966), pp. 398–407.

the value of the national forests. Amenity-seekers exerted pressure on policymakers to revise their priorities in favor of reserving forest lands for their uses. Policy decisions were increasingly forced into the open public arena and were no longer the sole domain of the omnipotent forester. Where the Forest Service previously dealt predominately with members of the forest products industry, they were now also faced with individuals concerned with recreational and aesthetic uses of the forest. Although many amenity-seekers would have it believed that their "use" entails no use, recreational and aesthetic amenities are, in a very real sense, outputs of the forest commons. Resources are expended toward their provision and use, i.e., they have an opportunity cost. As we shall see presently, these amenity outputs are essentially affected by individ-

**Figure 1.—Total Recreation Visits—All Sites***

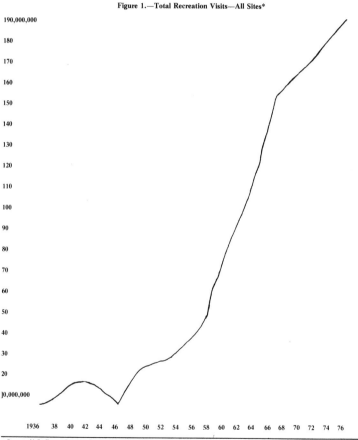

Source: U.S. Forest Service. Recreation Information Management Summaries.
*Accounting procedures were changed in 1965.

16

uals acting under the logic of the commons in a similar manner to those who seek commodities.

By the late sixties the preservation of free-flowing water courses, air-sheds, wildlife, and trees became the central endeavor of powerful amenity-seeking interest groups.[3] Related judicial actions developed as the courts expanded the rules of standing upon which citizens and groups could bring suit.[4]

Along with the courts, Congress responded to demands for greater natural resource protection. The Wilderness Act of 1964, the National Environmental Policy Act (NEPA) of 1969, and the National Forest Management Act of 1976 are major expressions of congressional concern over environmental matters. Such acts may be viewed as translations of the public's willingness to withhold their consent over many types of resource use. These acts also opened Forest Service policy to public scrutiny and provided avenues for greater public influence on decisions.

**Influence Reversal in the Rocky Mountain Region**

An informative example of competition over use of common pool resources is provided by regions I and IV of the National Forest System. These regions comprise the Northern Rocky Mountain States, excluding Colorado and Eastern Wyoming.

The Rocky Mountain forests are not among the nation's most productive timber areas. Biomass production is relatively insignificant compared to that in the Northwest and Southeast. From the standpoint of harvest there exists good evidence that much of the currently standing timber exhibits negative net worth.[5] Further evidence suggests that

---

[3]See William Tucker, "Environmentalism and the Leisure Class," *Harper's*, December, 1977, pp. 49–80.

[4]Landmark cases in this spirit include: *Scenic Hudson Preservation Conference v. Federal Power Commission*: 354 F.2d 608, (2d. Cir. 1965), Cert. denied 384 U.S. 941, (1966); *Sierra Club v. Morton*: 348 F. Supp. 219, (1972); *Environmental Defense Fund v. Environmental Protection Agency*: 150 App. D.C. 348, (1972); *Scientist's Institute for Public Information v. Atomic Energy Commission*: 156 U.S. App. D.C. 395, (1973); *Sierra Club v. Mason*: 351 F. Supp. 419, (D.C. Conn. 1972); *United States v. SCRAP*: 412 U.S. 669, 93 S. Ct. 2405, (1973). See William H. Rodgers Jr., *Handbook on Environmental Law*, (West Pub. Co. 1977), pp. 23–30 for incisive discussion of these cases and the expansion of standing, generally.

[5]Hyde, William F., "Compounding Clearcuts: The Failure of Public Timber Management in the Rockies," and Barney Dowdle, "An Institutional Dinosaur with An Ace: Or, How to Piddle Away Public Timber Wealth and Foul the Environment in the Process," both papers presented at the Liberty Fund Conference, Big Sky, Montana. Sept. 11–14, 1978.

much harvesting is completed at a financial loss subsidized out of the national treasury— another restricted common pool resource.[6]

Historically, actions and attitudes toward the forest lands of Regions I and IV can be described by three distinct developmental phases.[7] Because of long distances to principal markets the first phase, beginning before the turn of the century, was distinguished by an interest in only the most valuable high quality species. As a result of these practical limitations, only a small portion of the total timber resource was considered commercial.

Backlogged housing demands at the end of World War II and improvements in wood processing technology combined with transportation improvements to make previously non-merchantable species worth harvesting. As a result, logging became increasingly profitable and business boomed—the beginning of developmental stage two. The number of active sawmills in the area increased from 725 (in 1942) to 1107 (in 1974) and record volumes of timber were cut.[8]

Currently, the third developmental phase is characterized by an active concern for the recognition and protection of non-timber forest amenities. Much broader public attention is being focused upon non-timber uses and environmental impacts associated with timber growing and harvesting.

Not surprisingly, when timber harvest has a major impact on a local economy many local residents value it highly. In Regions I and IV the economic impact of timber harvesting has been decreasing since 1950 while, concurrent with the ORD in the nation-at-large, the influence of amenity-seekers has increased. Timber production increases since World War II, except in Utah (Table 1), have *not* resulted in increased employment. Labor involved in producing each unit of wood has dropped sharply due to technological advancement. Hence, due to pro-

---

[6]See Baden and Fort, "Natural Resources and Bureaucratic Predators," *Policy Review*, Winter, 1980, pp. 69–81. Common pool resources lack exclusivity of ownership. A large number of independent users have access rights and no users can control the actions of other users. These elements, contributing to the existence of a commons, exist in sufficient quantity that to label the portion of the tax base allocated to bureaucratic budgets as a commons is not indefensible.

Seeking to maximize his gain, each bureaucrat realizes his accessibility to the tax base. There are associated gain and cost components. The gain is unity (all of it goes to finance his agency's activities) and the costs of his capture are dispersed as lost opportunities for other bureaucrats. All bureaucrats realize the same individual calculus and it is rational for each to attempt to capture additional budget increments. That tragedy ensues is predictable but such a discussion is the basis for another paper.

[7]Alan W. Green and Theodore S. Setzer, "The Rocky Mountain Timber Situation, 1970," *USDA Forest Service Resource Bulletin INT-10* November, 1974, p. 304.

[8]U.S. Department of Commerce, *Bureau of the Census, Current Industrial Reports, Lumber Production and Mill Stocks*, 1942–1946.

## Table 1
## Lumber Production in Rocky Mountain States
## 1952–1976
## (in million board feet, lumber tally)

| Year | Wyoming | Idaho | Montana | Utah |
|---|---|---|---|---|
| 1952 | — | 1,106 | 702 | — |
| 1953 | — | 1,101 | 757 | — |
| 1954 | 81 | 1,399 | 738 | 51 |
| 1955 | — | 1,413 | 785 | — |
| 1956 | — | 1,608 | 981 | — |
| 1957 | 109 | 1,277 | 733 | — |
| 1958 | 105 | 1,437 | 924 | — |
| 1959 | 107 | 1,802 | 1,044 | — |
| 1960 | 99 | 1,405 | 985 | 69 |
| 1961 | 97 | 1,467 | 985 | 66 |
| 1962 | 103 | 1,516 | 1,069 | 67 |
| 1963 | 112 | 1,568 | 1,175 | 74 |
| 1964 | 132 | 1,656 | 1,221 | 69 |
| 1965 | 135 | 1,674 | 1,308 | 64 |
| 1966 | 125 | 1,601 | 1,377 | 72 |
| 1967 | 155 | 1,649 | 1,350 | 70 |
| 1968 | 174 | 1,686 | 1,497 | 67 |
| 1969 | Not available | | | |
| 1970 | 178 | 1,701 | 1,502 | 71 |
| 1971 | 217 | 1,720 | 1,494 | 56 |
| 1972 | 241 | 1,763 | 1,370 | 60 |
| 1973 | 251 | 1,863 | 1,484 | 54 |
| 1974 | 188 | 1,619 | 1,209 | 54 |
| 1975 | 175 | 1,723 | 1,122 | 52 |
| 1976 | 226 | 1,939 | 1,376 | 64 |

Source: U.S. Department of Commerce, *Bureau of the Census, Current Industrial Reports, Lumber Production and Mill Stocks,* 1952-1976.

duction and population increases (Table 2), the number of persons as well as the proportion of the population involved in timber activities dropped over the time period when the influence of amenity-seekers achieved its most significant gains (Table 3).

A second major factor behind the rising influence of amenity-seekers was the shift in the ownership patterns of local logging and mill operations. Many of the mills at this time were small family-type operations typically processing less than one million board feet annually. A 1954 Census Bureau survey reveals that sixty-two percent of all sawmills in Regions I and IV were in this category. The size of logging operations corresponded to sawmill size; logging operations were relatively small.

In the period 1950–1970 many of the smaller mills closed (see Table 4). One reason was comparative disadvantage against larger, more mechanized mills. Often, however, Forest Service timber sales were in such large parcels that smaller family operations were simply incapable

19

**Table 2**

**Rocky Mountain States Population Statistics**

| | Montana | | | Idaho | | | Wyoming | | | Utah | | |
|---|---|---|---|---|---|---|---|---|---|---|---|---|
| | % Pop. Urban | Total Pop. | % increase | % Pop. Urban | Total Pop. | % increase | % Pop. Urban | Total Pop. | % increase | % Pop. Urban | Total Pop. | % increase |
| 1930 | 33.7 | 537,606 | | 29.1 | 445,032 | | 31.1 | 225,565 | | 52.4 | 507,847 | |
| 1940 | 37.8 | 559,456 | 4.1 | 33.7 | 524,873 | 17.9 | 37.3 | 250,742 | 11.2 | 55.5 | 550,310 | 8.4 |
| 1950 | 43.7 | 591,024 | 5.6 | 42.9 | 588,637 | 12.1 | 49.8 | 290,529 | 15.9 | 63.3 | 688,862 | 25.2 |
| 1960 | 50.2 | 674,767 | 14.2 | 47.5 | 667,191 | 13.3 | 56.8 | 330,066 | 13.6 | 74.9 | 890,627 | 29.3 |
| 1970 | 53.4 | 694,409 | 2.9 | 54.1 | 712,567 | 6.8 | 60.5 | 332,416 | 0.7 | 80.4 | 1,059,273 | 18.9 |

Source: U.S. Department of Commerce, *Bureau of the Census, Population Characteristics,* 1930-1970.

20

### Table 3
### Population Employed in Logging
### 1940–1970

| | Montana | | Idaho | | Wyoming | | Utah | |
|---|---|---|---|---|---|---|---|---|
| | N | % of Total Population | N | % | N | % | N | % |
| 1940 | 1,021 | .182 | 2,063 | .393 | 242 | .097 | 72 | .013 |
| 1950 | 1,112 | .188 | 2,251 | .382 | 265 | .091 | 80 | .011 |
| 1960 | 860 | .127 | 1,262 | .189 | 126 | .038 | 81 | .009 |
| 1970 | 692 | .01 | 586 | .082 | 123 | .037 | 59 | .006 |

Source: U.S. Department of Commerce, *Bureau of the Census, Population Characteristics,* 1940–1970.

### Table 4
### Numbers of Active Sawmills in the Rocky Mountain States

| Year | Small Mills* | Medium Mills* | Large Mills* | Total Mills |
|---|---|---|---|---|
| 1942 | Not available | Not available | Not available | 725 |
| 1946 | 898 | 169 | 19 | 1,086 |
| 1954 | 336 | 157 | 52 | 545 |
| 1966 | 242 | 101 | 88 | 431 |

Source: U.S. Department of Commerce, *Bureau of the Census, Current Industrial Reports, Lumber Production and Mill Stocks,* 1942–1970.

of processing the volume of timber involved even if they were financially able to bid. Most were not. The result was either mill closure or purchase by outside corporations which transferred ownership outside of the region.

As mills closed and ownership was transferred outside of the regions, as mechanization allowed greater harvest and processing with fewer men, and as those employed in timber activities became increasingly transient, the timber industry's effect on local economies diminished greatly. Region I and IV residents lost a direct economic stake in continued timber harvest. More important for this discussion, since everyday interactions between foresters and mill operators and employees no longer involved local residents with strong community ties, the influence of those interested in timber harvest was rapidly displaced by the growing influence of ORD participants. Figure 3 shows the tremendous increase in visits to the national forests in Regions I and IV.

An examination of forest recreation statistics reveals that "general enjoyment" and "sightseeing" are the major pursuits of amenity-

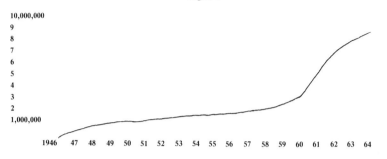

Figure 3.—Total Recreation Visits all Sites
Region I

Source: U.S. Department of Agriculture, U.S. Forest Service 2300-1 Annual Statistical Report, 1940-1964

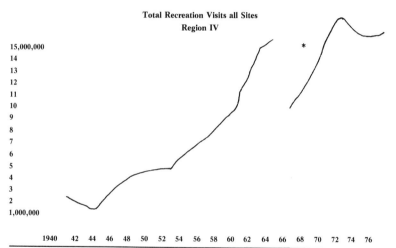

Total Recreation Visits all Sites
Region IV

Source: U.S. Department of Agriculture, *U.S. Forest Service, Recreation Information Management (RIM), Recreation Use Statistics,* 1977.
*Accounting Procedures changed in 1965.

seekers.[9] These activities received a substantial technological boost with the advent of such recreational vehicles as four-wheel drives, trail bikes, and snowmobiles which have increased accessibility to the back country. Other forms of transportation satisfy the needs of amenity-seekers opposed to the mechanized aspects of the ORD—hiking, back-packing, and cross-country skiing.[10] Whether the orientation is toward

---

[9]*Recreation Information Management (RIM), Recreation Use Statistics,* USDA Forest Service, 1977.
[10]See John Baden, "Neospartan Hedonists, Adult Toy Aficionados, and the Rationing of Public Lands," in *Managing the Commons,* Garrett Hardin and John Baden (eds.), pp. 241-251.

22

fine-tuning oneself or one's machine, preserving forests for recreation has become paramount to many members of concentrated interest groups.

## Impact of ORD on Harvest Practices in Regions I and IV

The reduction of timber harvest impacts and increased environmental awareness through forest recreation have combined to focus attention upon timber management practices in the Rocky Mountain States. Where the previous major issue was balance of cut and growth, the issues now considered by the public include demands for environmental constraints on many harvest practices. Since the late sixties, there has been mounting public pressure to place higher priority on watershed, wildlife, recreation, and scenic values than ever before.

Nationally, public pressure on Congress resulted in the National Environmental Policy Act (NEPA) of 1969. The effect of the Act in Region I was that, regardless of changes in industry utilization standards resulting in upward revisions of allowable sawtimber cut, the actual removals have averaged some 200 million board feet below the allowable since 1969.[11] One reason has been slowed contract letting due to the National Environmental Policy Act's mandated impact statements for individual timber sales. The result is that timber sales dropped substantially following the enactment of NEPA.

Clearcutting, a harvest method used frequently in Regions I and IV, is a focal point of public concern. Until the mid-sixties, harvest plans were often laid out in convenient but ecologically arbitrary straightline boundaries, sometimes even following section lines. These clearcuts resulted in rectangles and other shapes that largely ignored the relation of the cutting to terrain and sometimes exceeded 1000 acres.[12]

The visual impact of clearcutting, especially in square parcels, outraged the recreational public. Subsequently, regional directives instructed Supervisors, Rangers, and timber staffers to consider alternative methods of harvest.[13] By 1970, harvest plans followed contour lines which developed into natural looking meadows. Subsequent management plans generally limit clearcuts to a maximum of thirty-five to forty acres. Current plans often call for light selection cutting,

---

[11]Green and Setzer, p. 21.
[12]*Forest Management in Wyoming: Timber Harvest and the Environment on the Teton, Bridger, Shoshone, and Bighorn National Forests,* Forest Service: U.S. Department of Agriculture, 1971, 17-28.
[13]*Ibid.,* p. 14.

particularly on the low-yielding timber sites. This method removes some mature trees and has been tabbed "pussyfoot logging" because the logger would leave few tracks.[14] Such plans call for small clearcuts of just five to ten acres. Another harvest practice is the "nibbling" technique in which certain cuttings are pared from timber stands adjacent to sage or aspen areas or the perimeter of existent openings.[15] This technique results in a low visual impact as it takes advantage of natural patterns at the stand margins.

Alternative harvest methods have also imposed substantial administrative costs on the Forest Service due to the increased detail and time spent per unit area for sale preparation, silvicultural prescriptions, and sale administration.

### Logic of the Commons and the Activities of ORD Participants

One well known tool applicable to the examination of ORD participants' behavior in the Rocky Mountain States is the model developed by Garrett Hardin in "The Tragedy of the Commons."[16] Following some basic assumptions concerning self-interested behavior motivation he suggests that individuals in a non-exclusive, undefined property rights institutional setting—not at all unlike the restricted national forests commons—will maximize private benefits while ignoring any negative impacts their actions have on others. Moreover, they will continue to do so until the private marginal benefits just equal the private marginal costs of production. In his 1968 article, Hardin presents an analogy between the human environment and a common pasture to which all users have equal access. Several herdsmen graze their animals on the commons free of charge and each herdsman may put as many animals on the pasture as he sees fit. So long as the total number of animals is below the carrying capacity of the commons, a herdsman can add an animal to his herd without affecting the amount of grazing for any animals including his own. But beyond this point, the addition of another animal has negative consequences for all users of the common pasture including the herdsman. A rational herdsman, seeing that the benefit obtained from the additional animal accrues entirely to himself but that the effects of overgrazing are shared by all the herdsmen, adds

---

[14]*Ibid.,* pp. 14–15.

[15]*Ibid.,* pp. 31–32.

[16]Garrett Hardin, "The Tragedy of the Commons," *Science,* 162, 1968, pp. 1243–1248.

24

an animal to the commons. For the same reason, he decides to continue adding animals, as do the other herdsmen. Each, through an individual calculus, realizes that if he refrains from adding the additional animals, he will have to absorb a greater share of the external costs generated by the maximizing herdsmen. He becomes a "sucker" while others obtain an essentially free ride at his expense. The process of adding animals may continue until the ability of the commons to support livestock collapses entirely. Empirical evidence such as the West African Sahel stand in awesome testimony of the validity of the "logic of the commons." It should be noted that an individual herdsman acting alone cannot save the common through his own actions since he is not alone in endangering it. Unilateral restraint only assures a herdsman a smaller herd, not a stable pasture. The "tragedy of the commons" is not simply the fact that the commons is destroyed, but that rational individual action may produce consequences that leave everyone worse off.

In a true commons, the right to free access by one user cannot be restricted by other users. In this sense, the national forests cannot be considered a strictly defined commons. The Forest Service was created to restrict use of the forests. Further access restrictions may arise from proximity differences and variations in discretionary time. Also, not every citizen or group receives equal weight in the allocation process. However, various groups with mutually exclusive goals do have as direct access as possible and these can be considered the users of the restricted forest commons. To produce a "tragedy of the commons" it is *not* necessary that each herdsman possess an equal ability to exploit the commons. Those unable to exploit the commons as fully as others simply become unwilling victims who must disproportionately bear the costs imposed on the community by those granted the ability to exploit. The dictates of self-interest maximization continue to result in a divergence of individual behavior away from the summed welfare of the members of the society. Hardin's analysis is valuable to the extent that it can accurately describe and predict present and future outcomes under even restricted commons situations.

Those individuals viewing local forests as recreational and scenic "amenity-sheds" are like individual herdsmen in the common pasture. It is sensible to each and every "amenities-herdsman" to attempt to maximize amenities output on the national forests regardless of the external cost distributed over the entire community of users. These costs are generally disemployment and higher wood product prices. The amenities-shed with which they are concerned provides benefits which

25

are captured locally, typically within a 100 mile radius.[17] So, while individual amenity-seekers do not bear the complete costs of their amenity-seeking activities, substantial recreational and scenic benefits are concentrated locally.

It should be noted that if *all* amenity-seekers follow the same logic in an attempt to capture the available benefits, as the logic of the commons dictates they will, then the potential for socially non-optimal outcomes increases. The commons model demonstrates how amenity-seekers, acting in their own self-interest, can produce social consequences which are optimal *only if social gains from preserving a timber stand are greater than the gains from its harvest.* A quandry lies in comparing recreational and aesthetic values, which are not specified by any market price structure, to wood product values which are market priced.

## CONCLUSION

Many timber sales in the Rockies are subsidized, i.e., the cost of administering the sale and harvesting the timber exceeds the value of the logs. If the resources were in private hands such sales would not occur. These sales enhance efficiency to the degree that the amenity-seekers prevent them from occurring. It is obvious, however, that managerial efficiency is not the amenity-seekers' primary goal. Rather, members of this group act as self-interested contenders for a publicly controlled resource. Some factors influencing current public attitudes appear to

---

[17]"For all kinds of outdoor recreation areas, a distance-decay function is strongly operative; that is, the proportion of people visiting an area, and the frequency of their visits, declines rapidly as distance from the area increases...and it seems probable that the overwhelming majority of the visitors to national forests live within 100 miles of the forest they visit...To this extent, the benefits of national forest outdoor recreation are more regional and local, and less national, than are the benefits of either their wood or their forage production, since the consumer products from the latter two outputs move nationally more than does the recreation output." Marion Clawson, "Economics of National Forest Management," Resources for the Future Working Paper EN-6, (Resources for the Future June 1976), p. 30. A specific comment concerning a similar distance-decay function for Wilderness Areas is made on p. 33. Knetsch also states that, "For most forms of recreation, the price factor on which demand depends is largely a variable measuring the relative availability in terms of locational proximity; people usually go more often to sites that are easily accessible." Jack L. Knetsch, "Outdoor Recreation and Water Resource Planning," Water Resources Monograph 3, (American Geophysical Union 1974), pp. 11–27. A review of the literature concerning the relationships of travel time and use is provided by Barry O'Rourke, "Travel in the Recreational Experience—A Literature Review," *Journal of Leisure Research*, 6 (Spring 1974): 140–156. Also, see Marion Clawson and Jack L. Knetsch, *Economics of Outdoor Recreation,* (Johns Hopkins Press, 1966), pp. 98–99; Robert W. Douglas, *Forest Recreation.* 2nd ed., (Pergamon Press, 1975), pp. 20–24; and Clayne R. Jensen, *Outdoor Recreation in America.* 3rd ed., Burgess Pub. Co., 1977, pp. 25–30.

be decreased economic dependence on logging activities due to declining employment and absentee mill ownership; increased leisure time, mobility; and high marginal tax rates which encourage many people to enter the forests in search of the untaxed benefits of recreation.

In the forests, recreationists encounter the forester whom they defrock of his omnipotent powers through a series of court tests, congressional acts, and administrative appeals. Their aim has been to stop logging altogether in many areas or, failing that, to force a substitution of "pussyfoot logging" for clearcutting.

Timber harvest plans on each of the forests in the Regions are being met with extreme hostility. This hostility is usually couched in environmental terms, but the underlying argument is that local recreation and scenic values are greater than timber values. Disagreement with the nature of consequences of timber management activities has caused delays and inefficiencies and often prevented any harvesting on local forests.

Amenity-seekers do not deny the necessity of wood products. Their desire is that the trees be harvested somewhere other than on their small portion of the continent's forest preserves. This reasoning has led amenity-seekers everywhere to pursue local forest preservation and they have been, in large part, successful in capturing locally the recreation and scenic amenities provided by an uncut forest.

While providing substantial local benefits, amenity protection has led to increased timber harvest costs, thereby boosting wood product prices for the nation of users. If the amenity market values have surpassed wood product values, the result is socially optimal. If, however, amenity values are less than timber values, the higher wood product prices fit the predictions of the common model as individual action has produced consequences that are socially non-optimal.

Since forest amenities are not marketed, the problem of quantifying their value is difficult at best. We are left, under current practices, without a definite measure of whether the product resulting from competing uses of our common pool resources is socially optimal.

The increased recreational and aesthetic use of the nation's forests has resulted in the forests being considered as "amenity-sheds" rather than solely as timber sheds. To the extent that the amenity-seekers' objective of maximizing recreational and aesthetic amenities at the expense of timber harvest activities is met, spillover costs in the form of higher wood prices and lost employment opportunities are produced. Perhaps this behavior can be rationalized on the basis that "wood products producers ignored the spillovers that they dumped on us long enough and now the tables have turned. It's time for payment in kind."

27

It is relatively easy to point the emotional finger of blame but much more difficult to recognize the actual culprit. *Due to the existence of an institutionally enforced commons situation,* amenity-seekers—like Hardin's rational herdsman and the consumer goods production-oriented timber harvest types which preceded them—maximize private benefits while ignoring spillover costs to the community of which they are a part. There will be no costless solution to this problem. Understanding the reason for the behavior is an important first step toward the eventual alignment of individual behavior with the total welfare of the members of society. The assumption that people, including recreationists are fundamentally self-interested again serves as a guide for predicting behavior.

## BIBLIOGRAPHY

Baden, John. "Neospartan Hedonists, Adult Toy Aficionados, and the Rationing of Public Lands," in *Managing the Commons,* Garrett Hardin and John Baden (eds.) (San Francisco: W. H. Freeman and Company, 1977).

Behan, R. W. "The Myth of the Omnipotent Forester," *Journal of Forestry,* Vol. 64, No. 6 (1966).

Clawson, Marion, "Economics of National Forest Management," Resources for the Future Working Paper EN-6 (Resources for the Future June, 1974).

Clawson, Marion, and Knetsch, Jack L., *Economics of Outdoor Recreation* (Johns Hopkins Press 1966).

*Current Industrial Reports.,* Bureau of the Census (1942-1946).

Douglas, Robert W., *Forest Recreation,* 2nd ed. (Pergamon Press 1975).

Dowdle, Barney, "An Institutional Dinosaur with An Ace: or, How to Piddle Away Public Timber Wealth and Foul the Environment in the Process," presented at the Liberty Fund Conference, Big Sky, Montana, Sept. 11-14, 1978. Soon to appear in a volume on Natural Resource Economic Policy forthcoming from The University of Michigan Press; Baden and Stroup, contributing editors.

Forest Management in Wyoming: Timber Harvest and the Environment on the Teton, Bridger, Shoshone, and Bighorn National Forests, Forest Service: U.S. Department of Agriculture (1971).

Green, Alan W., and Setzerm Theodore S. "The Rocky Mountain Timber Situation, 1970,: *USDA Forest Service Resource Bulletin INT-10* (1974).

Hardin, Garrett. "The Tragedy of the Commons," *Science,* 1968/162, 243-48.

Harry, Joseph; Gale, Richard; and Hendee, John. "Conservation: An Upper Middle Class Social Movement," *Journal of Leisure Research,* Vol. 1, No. 3 (Summer, 1969), pp. 246-254.

Hyde, William F., "Compounding Clearcuts: The Failure of Public Timber Management in the Rockies," presented at the Liberty Fund Conference, Big Sky, Montana, Sept. 11-14, 1978. Soon to appear in a volume on Natural Resource Economic Policy forthcoming from The University of Michigan Press; Baden and Stroup, contributing editors.

Jensen, Clayne R., *Outdoor Recreation in America,* 3rd ed., Burgess Pub. Co. (1977).

Kemper, Robert E., and Davis, Lawrence S. "Costs of Environmental Constraints on Timber Harvest and Regeneration," *Journal of Forestry,* Vol. 74, No. 11 (November, 1976).

Knetsch, Jack L., "Outdoor Recreation and Water Resource Planning," Water Resources Monograph 3 (American Geophysical Union 1974).

O'Rourke, Barry, "Travel in the Recreation Experience—A Literature Review," *Journal of Leisure Research,* 6 (Spring 1974): 140-156.

"RARE II: A Citizen's Handbook for the National Forest Roadless Area Review and Evaluation Program, 1977-1978," *Sierra Club National News Report* (November, 1977).

*Recreation Information Management, Recreation Use Statistics,* U.S. Forest Service, 1977.

Rodgers, William H., Jr., *Handbook on Environmental Law,* (West Pub. Co. 1977).

Tucker, William. "Environmentalism and the Leisure Class," *Harper's,* 225 (December, 1977).

William, Bob. "Management Philosophy Allows Use for All," *The Post Register,* Idaho Falls, Idaho (October, 1977).

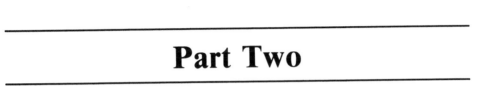

# Part Two

# 4

# Environmental Quality, Social Welfare and Bureaucratic Pathologies

## Introduction

As indicated above, in the early days of the environmental movement it was generally accepted that self-interest and the profit motive fostered environmental destruction. Rather than identifying the cause as poorly defined and defended property rights, i.e., a political and institutional failure, the market system was blamed. Thus a logical next step was to place increasing reliance upon bureaucratic solutions. Since bureaucrats do not obtain profits, the underlying motivation for environmental destruction would be absent. Reality, however, intrudes. Experience suggests that bureaucrats, like others, respond to incentives. Self-interest tends to dominate over considerations of environmental quality. As this section indicates, self-interest, *even in the absence of profits*, can still lead to excessively high environmental costs.

During the decade since Earth Day, a large and growing number of articles, technical reports, and books have developed the theme that large social benefits can be generated through increased governmental action, management, ownership, and control. This is especially true in the area of natural resource management. A strong distrust of private property as an institution coupled with increasing demands for scarce natural resources and greater environmental quality has led to more and stronger calls for more collective management to supplant or control what is viewed as the rapacious private exploitation of nature.

Privately held property rights in natural resources are increasingly attacked. This is due partly to concern over what many perceive to be an imbalance in the distribution of benefits from nature's bounty. It is also due in part to what is thought to be irresponsible stewardship of

Adapted from Baden and Stroup, "Environmental Costs of Government Action," *Policy Review*, Spring 1978.

natural resources in the pursuit of profits. Market failure is increasingly noted. Negative externalities, which are costs accruing to those other than the decisionmaker, frequently are cited as justification for the imposition of governmental control. The rule of willing consent is relaxed, and collective decisionmaking is imposed.

The market, based upon the willing consent of individuals and operating through the mechanism of prices representing condensed information and incentives, tends to move resources to the most highly valued uses. When transaction costs are negligible and property rights are clean and readily enforceable, the market will, given any existing distribution of income, provide the socially optimal production of goods and services. Unfortunately, when dealing with some natural resources, there are only very imperfect property rights, as witness clean air and clean water. Resources such as these tend to be underpriced. As a result, the production process generates not only goods but also evils in the form of negative externalities. Because environmental goods tend to be public goods and common pool resources, the private market will not efficiently utilize these resources. In principle, if the relevant parties are identified, injured individuals could collect damages through the courts using nuisance laws. However, transaction costs among a large number of disparate individuals are extremely high. Each tends to be a "free rider," not joining in legal action. Thus, to move toward the optimum allocation, the rule of willing consent is relaxed, and governmental mandates are imposed. Hence, great social benefits can potentially be generated via the imposition of government regulation and control. This has been the dominant theme of most of the political economy literature on environmental management.

There is, however, a set of environmental quality issues that has been relatively neglected by resource scholars. These issues involve reductions in environmental quality *generated* by the positive action of governmental agencies and are the subject of this section. It is easy for most of us to understand why profit-seeking individuals or firms will engage in environmentally destructive practices when they receive signals regarding the value of resource inputs which are faulty due to poorly defined property rights. A smaller proportion of people, however, have an intuitive understanding of why it is the case that bureaucrats, individuals whose salaries bear little or no relationship to profit, should engage in analogous behavior.

The root cause of failure in the collective and private arenas is the same: authority and responsibility are separated. In the private sector, this occurs when property rights are not clearly established and/or en-

34

forceable. For example, the smelter owner uses the air resource for free garbage ($SO_2$) removal, and is not held responsible. He captures benefits from use of the air but does not bear any costs of doing so. Similarly—but much more frequently—in the public sector, the individual with the authority to order an action does not bear certain important costs of that action. When the Federal Power Commission keeps natural gas wellhead prices low, for example, commissioners are applauded for protecting gas buyers. The commissioners are not condemned for causing the environmental damages due to extra electricity production, a multi-billion dollar Alaskan gas pipeline, or environmentally and economically expensive coal conversion to natural gas. These damages are promoted by their actions. And if the commissioners *were* blamed, the cost to them of condemnation would not approach the sum of the total costs to society. Better public decisions really are public goods.

In general, public sector activity suffers from what Hardin has labeled, in a non-governmental setting, the "tragedy of the commons." Everyone's property is no one's property. The public purse and public authority, like common pastures, are over-utilized for the benefit of the few at the cost of the many. Efficient management is elusive, hard to recognize when users do not pay, and seldom attained. Further, an equal sharing of public benefits and costs is impossible even with one-man-one-vote democracy. A lucky few will enjoy the water from federally financed water projects, artificially cheap natural gas, or the extra forage produced by the chaining of pinyon-juniper stands. Yet all incur the costs. The ability to influence government is probably no more (and arguably less) equally distributed than the money income which can influence market decisions. Yet, when concentrated "special" interest groups are found to wield power in obtaining large governmental benefits, specific people are usually seen as the cause of the problem. We argue that the system's *structure*, not evil individuals, can best explain such problems. Because of the difference in property rights, the same frontier white men who nearly wiped out the buffalo posed no threat to the more valuable beef cattle raised on the western range. Similarly, better institutional arrangements can better channel the efforts of imperfect men, the vast majority of whom could never be considered seriously for sainthood.

In this section, we intend to 1) explain, using common-sense elements of the property rights paradigm and public choice theory, why we should not *expect* collective management to provide either careful stewardship *or* a balanced reflection of public desires; 2) present examples of how this logic reflects the real world, so that collective manage-

35

ment, usually thought to be the solution, is in fact often the problem; and 3) provide the analytical foundations for developing private institutions and revising public institutions to foster efficient and non-coercive stewardship of natural environments.

## The Framework of Analysis

In predicting or analyzing public sector behavior, the appropriate unit of analysis is the individual decisionmaker. We must also recognize that we operate in a representative democracy, not a townmeeting democracy. At the national level politicians and bureaucrats are in control and the average citizen knows little in detail about most government operations. In most of the cases that follow (and probably in most important cases), the key decisionmaker is the professional public servant—the bureaucrat.

Bureaucrats, like most other people, are largely self-interested. Like the rest of us, they will sometimes act altruistically to advance the public interest. In most work-related situations, however, a bureaucrat will act in such a manner as to improve his own welfare. The components of a bureaucrat's welfare include salary, relative position in the agency, discretionary control over budget, perquisites of office, and work place amenities. The nature of the world is such that these components of welfare are improved as the agency grows. Conversely, reduction of welfare tends to be associated with the contraction of an agency. Thus, decisionmakers within an agency face strong incentives to continually expand the scope of their agency's activities.[1]

Unlike their counterparts in the private sector, the expansionary activities undertaken by agencies need not generate value that exceeds cost. Because their budget is derived from taxes rather than the sale of products, bureaucrats have incentives to ignore or exaggerate the economic efficiency of the various projects that they propose, sponsor, and administer. Within this context the creative bureaucratic entrepreneur can identify a specific clientele that stands to benefit from the proposed action. In exchange for strong political support for his agency, he can finance this action with a subsidy from the general taxpayer. Hence, from the perspective of the bureaucrat, the tax base becomes a com-

[1]Variations on this theme are presented in T. E. Borcherding, ed., *Budgets and Bureaucrats: The Sources of Government Growth* (Durham, N.C.: Duke University Press, 1977), R. B. McKenzie and G. Tullock, *Modern Political Economy* (N.Y.: McGraw-Hill, 1978); and W. A. Niskanen, Jr., *Bureaucracy and Representative Government* (Chicago: Aldine-Atherton, 1971), among other sources.

mon pool resource ripe for exploitation. In contrast, the private individual or firm will not intentionally overproduce goods when the social value of the inputs is accurately reflected in the price of these inputs. The bureaucrat can ignore the foregone value of inputs. Hence, he will over-produce dams, grass, timber, and a host of other goods because the resources used in the production (tax money or timberland), are tapped from a common pool resource.

In a representative democracy, bureaucratic discretion and its abuse are possible because of voters' rational ignorance.[2] Sometimes mistaken for simple apathy, the average voter's lack of diligence in learning about and trying to control agency behavior is easily explained by his lack of individual control as well as the *opportunity cost* of obtaining information. A given resource management activity may mean far more to a voter than where he buys his gasoline. Yet all the benefits of knowing where to buy gas are his and he controls the decision. Whether pinyon-juniper stands will be chained is normally beyond his control. His learning time buys him more in shopping for gas than in learning about the Bureau of Land Management or Forest Service policy. He is rationally ignorant about most important policy issues. Those with concentrated interests in a particular resource are not and their marginal influence typically controls.

Most, if not all, of the environmentally destructive practices discussed in what follows would not occur if the agencies were required to meet the standards of economic efficiency. In effect, the general taxpayer often finds himself subsidizing the destruction of the American environment while making transfer payments to bureaucrats and highly specific special interests. Thus, there are huge social profits to be made by explicating and advertising this situation and constraining the activities of the agencies discussed.

Those who stand to benefit from constraints being imposed upon excessive governmental action are numerous indeed. Obviously, the general taxpayer is advantaged if the government operates in a manner consistent with economic efficiency. Environmentalists should welcome a reduction in governmental programs that fail to meet the tests of economic efficiency and are demonstrably destructive of the environment. Such programs convert relatively pristine environments into chained, terraced, dammed, flooded, channelized, and similarly disturbed areas. Hopefully, most Americans would agree that we should engage

<hr>

[2]Rational ignorance and other problems in collective decision-making are discussed in J. D. Gwartney, *Economics: Private and Public Choice* (N.Y.: Academic Press, 1976) and in R. B. McKenzie and G. Tullock, *op.cit.*

in development when the net benefits exceed the costs and that we should stop *subsidizing* the destruction of nature.

A third category of those likely to support careful analysis of governmental actions are those of us who view freedom as a scarce and very valuable resource and who realize that the growth of government, whatever the benefits, constitutes an extraordinarily serious, pervasive, and unavoidable threat to that resource.

The groups discussed above are not mutually exclusive. All of us are taxpayers, many of us are environmentalists, and some of us set a very high value on freedom. The conjunction is not insignificant and we are hopeful that the number is growing. One of our colleagues, in discussing this same problem, has likened a land management agency to the Titanic steaming through the night. This section serves as a warning to the agencies that icebergs lie ahead. We hope they will heed these warnings. If they do not, the public is likely to raise the decibels of the message. The cases are strong; the evidence is clear. The public, we feel, is increasingly receptive to the kind of analysis presented here.

**Case Studies of Good Intentions Gone Astray**

The staffs of our land and resource management agencies tend to be competent and well-meaning. Most, in fact, are concerned and knowledgeable about the resources they manage. This conjunction, although fortunate, is by no means sufficient to insure quality management. There are, unfortunately, many examples of perverse institutional structures generating suboptimal results. We will introduce a few examples and then present an overview of two cases.

The U.S. Forest Service administers vast stands of timber in the western United States. Some of this timber land, notably that in northern California and western Oregon and Washington, is extremely productive. In contrast, the land in the Rocky Mountain States is much less productive *for growing trees as a crop*. Its uses are largely recreational and aesthetic which are also of high value. Silvicultural treatments (such as clearcutting) on many of these high, dry, and ecologically fragile sites are often destructive of other forest values. In essence, these are tradeoffs between timber management and management for other valued uses. This situation, of course, is neither surprising nor necessarily socially costly. Unfortunately, however, in the less productive regions, much of this timber literally has a *negative value* as timber. In brief, the resources employed to extract the timber are often worth more than the timber harvested. It is only because this process is so heavily subsidized that massive ecological disturbances are undertaken.

In addition to forest lands, the West has vast areas of grazing or range land. Much of this cow country is administered by the Bureau of Land Management (BLM). This is land of such marginal productivity that it was not patented under the various homestead acts. Its productivity is so low that it commonly takes from ten to forty or more acres to carry a cow with calf for one month. With relatively large investments in fencing, water development, and seeding, the forage productivity of the land can be increased. Thus, the number of animal unit months generated can be expanded. One such management practice advocated by the BLM is called rest-rotation grazing. While it *may* indeed improve the range, this outcome is uncertain at best. Further, rest-rotation grazing fundamentally transforms the ecological system. Central to our argument, however, is the simple fact that this management practice is relatively capital and management intensive. Only under the most optimistic assumptions can it be expected to pay its own way. Massive subsidies are required if this transformation is to be made on the marginal range lands. Again we encounter an example of governmental assistance required for the economically inefficient modification of environments.

Water is a limiting factor in much of the western United States. Beyond the 100th meridian, agriculture is marginal or uncertain in the absence of irrigation. Hence, there may be great social benefits associated with the development of irrigation based on damming rivers. Unfortunately, we again confront a tradeoff: a section of river can be wild and scenic *or* it can be developed with dams and irrigation canals—only rarely can it be both. Clearly, those who stand to benefit from irrigation water will tend to favor development of a river. Thus, we should now consider the first law of demand which is the social analogue to the law of the gravity. Although irrigation water is valuable to those who use it, demand will cease when the marginal cost to the demander exceeds its marginal value. Unfortunately, governmental subsidies of water developments distort the prices faced by irrigators. Given that they confront water prices that are only a fraction of the real costs, their demand for water is much higher than it would be in the absence of subsidies. Thus, given that one set of interests is concentrated, there is a tremendous pressure to convert wild and scenic rivers to dammed and developed ones.

The absence of private property rights and direct government action in natural resources result in adverse environmental conditions. Notable examples include the over-grazing of the western Great Plains by cattlemen on the public lands. This practice destroyed the fragile ecological balance of the grasslands and thereby ultimately prepared the way for the "dust bowl." Private property rights were never extended into this area and the land was retained as open range within the public domain. The cattlemen, and later the sheepmen, were driven by economic incentives to over-graze before someone else did, and to graze too early in the year before the young grasses matured and seeded. Equally there was no incentive for any individual user to reseed over-grazed areas or to attempt any form of irrigation. Similar conditions still prevail on BLM lands where cattlemen and sheepmen can graze their animals at fees below what they would pay on private land, as well as upon land they do not own and may not be able to use the next year. Under these conditions, they have diminished incentives not to over-graze.

Most of the world's oceans fall into a similar category. With the absence of private ownership of most of the fishery resources (fish, shellfish, and whales) there has been a continuous saga of one species after another being over-harvested. No individual user has had any economic incentive not to over-use the resource. One may compare this with the rational conservation practices carried out in private farming operations for fish and shellfish.[3]

These cases are cited briefly here merely as examples of a general occurrence and illustrate the range of the problem. We can expect the conjunction of highly special interests (bureaucracies and user groups) and a diffuse general public to hold sway over the development of our natural resources in the public sector.

## The Analytical Foundations for Better Resource Management

The property rights paradigm helps us to pinpoint the cause of environmental problems in a market setting: resource prices are distorted when property rights to a resource are not enforced. Those with the authority to increase social welfare are not forced to be responsible for their actions. We should not expect environmental problems to be solved automatically when we give up the rule of willing consent and opt for collective action. Indeed, we are likely to create environmental and other problems. The examples discussed above illustrate how it can

---

[3]See James A. Wilson, "A Test of the Tragedy of the Commons" in Garrett Hardin and John Baden, *Managing the Commons* (San Francisco: W. H. Freeman Press, 1977), pp. 96–111.

easily happen that even well-intentioned public servants are apt to cause problems when the feedback data and reality checks inherent in the price system are lacking.

Three steps seem likely candidates in the search for systematic improvement. First, we must recognize the problem. The separation of authority from responsibility, all too prevalent in the private sector, is normal in the public sector. What efficiency experts might call a lack of accountability results. Second, we must accept an imperfect solution: market failures do not automatically imply that collective action is better.[4] An imperfect market may actually be the best available alternative. Third, we use whatever insights we have to the incentives and information people face in alternative institutional arrangements and restructure those institutions. The authors have elsewhere explored some of these institutional alternatives in the case of forest management.[5] The potential payoffs of more work on the political economy of managing natural environments are indeed large. The case studies that follow represent some of this work.

---

[4]Of course the opposite also is true: an imperfection in collective management should not automatically cause us to avoid governmental action. The grass is *not* always greener.

The fate of the environment under a collectivist system has recently been explored in three studies: Fred Singleton, ed., *Environmental Misuse in the Soviet Union* (New York: Praeger Publishers, 1976), Phillip R. Pryde, *Conservation in the Soviet Union* (New York: Cambridge University Press, 1972), and Marshall I. Goldman, *The Spoils of Progress: Environmental Pollution in the Soviet Union* (Cambridge: MIT Press, 1972). These books were reviewed in *Policy Review*, Fall 1977 by Robert J. Smith.

[5]See R. L. Stroup and J. A. Baden, "Externality, Property Rights, and the Management of Our National Forests," *Journal of Law and Economics*, Vol. XVI, Spring 1973 and J. A. Baden and R. L. Stroup, "Private Rights, Public Choices, and the Management of National Forests," *Western Wildlands* (University of Montana, Missoula), Autumn, 1975.

# 5

## Compounding Clearcuts: The Social Failures of Public Timber Management in the Rockies

A great demand for railroad ties and mine props made logging practical and profitable in the plentiful virgin forests of 19th century Colorado. The dry Colorado climate is not conducive to regeneration. A century later grass and bush still cover many harvested areas. Colorado advertised by John Denver, *et al.*, faces an influx of people known for their recreational forest demands. This paper will discuss how these competing demands for limited forest resources (forest products vs. recreation) are failing to be met. It then suggests alternative forestry management programs that would be more economically efficient and less environmentally damaging than the existing Forest Service programs.

High social costs, such as clogged streams and eroded land, resulted from early logging practices throughout the United States. Such costs, plus early public concern over a perceived market failure in the lumber industry, led to the creation of a national forest system. The U.S. Forest Service today administers twenty percent of the nation's commercial forestland under a "sustained yield-even flow" mandate.

Under an ideal "sustained yield-even flow" forest management program, the Forest Service harvests and grows timber at the same rate. Thus, in principle the amount harvested annually equals the annual growth. The Forest Service's harvest and investment analysis includes three independent elements: 1) the decision on how much land is in the timber base; 2) the decision on when timber is "mature"; and, 3) the decision on how much mature timber to harvest and hence how much

This paper is a shortened adaptation by Kay Blemker of a paper with the same title presented at the September 1978 Liberty Fund-L.P.E.N.R. Conference on the Environmental Costs of Bureaucratic Government. William F. Hyde is the author of the original paper.

to invest in timber regrowth. The timberland base is defined as all commercial "productive" forestland, or that which produces approximately twenty cubic feet per acre of naturally grown fiber annually. It excludes land reserved for wilderness, scenic, and geologic areas, administrative sites, and so forth.

There is convincing evidence that it is economically infeasible to log some of the classified "commercially productive" forestland. In brief, the cost of logging exceeds the value of the product. Under these circumstances the Forest Service over-invests in timber production and simultaneously induces environmental damage in fragile ecological areas while precluding use of the terrain for many recreational opportunities.

Why does the Forest Service engage in such practices—practices that many consider inimical to its fundamental purpose? This behavior can be partially explained by the timber maturity decision criteria and "sustained yield-even flow" forest management. Timber that is ready for harvesting is "mature" or ripe. Private timber operators determine financial maturity as a function of expected stumpage receipts, management costs, and opportunity costs, the best alternative use of funds as determined by the discount rate. These private operators harvest when the net revenues exceed the discounted expected net revenues from delaying harvests one year. Only when the discount rate is zero and the timberland economically productive are the two definitions concurrent. Under the Forest Service definition of maturity, timber usually must be older and larger than the economically efficient private optimum before it is harvested.

After public foresters determine the timberland base or "commercial productive" forestland and the "proper" maturity age, they make harvest and investment decisions based in part on inventories of mature timber. As explained earlier, sustained yield requires annual harvests to equal average annual growth. Yet excess mature timber inventories provide for an annual "even flow" of *volume* from year to year, since most forests are years, and sometimes decades, from being regulated. Harvest increases, which can originate only from excess mature timber inventories, justify an increase in investments. However, the Forest Service applies sustained yield-even flow to its entire timber resources, *without* regard for large variances in land productivity. Wise harvest decisions in one location may finance and mask unwise investment decisions in another. This practice is analogous to Yves St. Laurent opening a shop in Circle, Montana, because business is flourishing in Palm Beach. Economical management would consider harvest and investment decisions on each parcel independently, calculating expected net financial returns instead of volume returns.

Public foresters appraise potential harvestable parcels. If the price exceeds an arbitrary minimum base price, they auction the timber to the highest bidder. Almost any positive assessment exceeds the short-term costs of building roads to the timber and administering timber sales. The Forest Service appraised price does not incorporate long run costs, which cover all the expenses of timber management over the full timber growing period.

A private timber producer might make the sale and use the sale price to guide reinvestment decisions. If the expected net revenues calculated from the sale price are insufficient to cover *short* and *long* run costs, he may cut losses after the first sale and bow out of the timber industry— or go bankrupt. The Federal law prohibits the Forest Service from selling its land, but it can allocate land to other uses. If no other use provides a positive rent, the Forest Service may act as a permanent caretaker of a forest ecosystem instead of a timber producer.

The revenue from additional sales of excess mature timber protects the Forest Service from unrewarding harvest and investment decisions by "balancing" losses from inefficient and environmentally harmful logging on unproductive timber parcels. It appears that the Forest Service delays harvesting all of the excess mature timber beyond the economically optimum age. Instead they prefer to use it gradually over the years to finance overinvestment in unproductive timberland to the detriment of environmental and recreational values. A case study of San Juan National Forest in southwestern Colorado confirms the contention that either private ownership or public management according to market efficiency criteria would provide *both* more lumber and environmental benefits at levels more closely approximating their social optima than does present public forest management.

San Juan National Forest comprises 1.85 million acres in a mountainous area of southwestern Colorado where the local economy depends largely on tourism and ranching. The isolation of the area restricts both recreational activities and timber production, although some logging continues for sawmills in two local towns with a combined population of 12,000.

Over the years the San Juan National Forest has supplied these local mills with virgin Ponderosa pine. However, as these stands are depleted, harvests progress up the mountainsides to include greater proportions of the less valuable Engelmann spruce, with small amounts of Aspen and Douglas fir.

Harvests of fifty-five to seventy percent Engelmann spruce have averaged 70 million board feet (MMbf) per year in recent years. Yet annual timber sales average less than 50 million board feet because large sales made in 1963 have only recently reached the mill. Despite appeals from the Wilderness Society and the Colorado Open Space Council, the Forest Service plans to maintain harvest levels of 70 MMbf and over by harvesting four large and fifteen smaller "marginal-access" and "marginal logging" areas within the next five years. "Marginal-access" timber logging roads cost more to build than the value of the standing timber, and "marginal-logging" areas possess ecologically fragile soil or topographic conditions that require expensive balloon, helicopter, or long cable logging systems to prevent environmental degradation.

Thirty percent of the timber offered for sale in the past five years has not even received bids. Yet the Forest Service plans to expand harvest levels from 70 MMbf to 125 MMbf, which will require 1,130 miles of new roads, including 570 miles on marginal-access lands, and another 1,285 existing miles upgraded for logging. Hyde's case study (detailed in his Conference Paper) confirms that expected revenues from the planned harvests do not even cover the short-run costs of building roads and administering the sales, much less the long-run costs of reforesting and managing these environmentally fragile areas.

Timber management costs on *currently managed lands* exceed expected stumpage receipts in all but the extreme case when all nontimber compatible forest resources are charged with administrative and protection costs that are common to timber and its compatible uses. Even this case is dubious, because the costs of foregone land opportunities such as hunting, fishing, camping, skiing, etc. were ignored. If these conflicting nontimber resources have positive net value, then they provide an argument for additional restrictions on public timber management.

The Forest Service, which was created to prevent an expected long-run timber shortage and provide for nonmarket forest values such as wilderness recreation, actually uses more land and capital in producing timber than is justified by market criteria. They do so to the detriment of amenity-valued non-market resources. The Forest Service supports these inefficient and detrimental practices through a 500 million dollar (and growing) annual deficit. Since the stumpage prices fail to reflect the actual logging costs, current subsidized public timber production levels depress the return of more efficient timber producers in other locations by artificially decreasing the stumpage prices. The planned expansion of timber harvests in San Juan National Forest would augment these negative effects.

Environmentalists appealed the expansion of San Juan National Forest on the efficiency grounds reviewed above. The Regional Forester granted the appeal, but the segment of the timber industry that benefits from the subsidies reappealed to the Chief of Forest Services in Washington, where the decision now rests.

The Forest Service resists reducing current inefficient harvest levels on the grounds that it has a responsibility to maintain local community stability. The Beaverhead National Forest in western Montana intends to continue harvesting despite a *Forest Service* calculated benefit-cost ratio of 0.37:1. Unless the Forest Service continues subsidizing forever, local unemployment of labor and capital is inevitable. The transition costs can hardly justify the perpetual inefficiency and nontimber values foregone, which might be more beneficial to the community stability in the long-run. Because of increasing rural land values and an increasing demand for recreational forest resources, it would make more sense to gradually cut back harvesting so that the local economy could gradually adjust and develop alternatives. If procrastination lasts until all of the timber is depleted, the community will face a sudden, drastic unemployment of labor and capital—and unprecedented instability. Moreover, applying efficiency criteria to all marginal public forestlands might reduce timber harvests sufficiently to create a price increasing effect. The new, higher price would make some marginal lands efficient timber producers, thus partially offsetting predicted local unemployment.

Perhaps because of evidence such as this, the Forest Service is beginning to respond affirmatively to efficiency criteria and to nonmarket values. Harvest levels have been reduced on some forests of the Southwest and the new Regional Forester in Denver is urging stricter justification of timber management. In both cases there are obvious and immediate gains to environmental protection and recreational values. Most important, the Forest Service has initiated a functional accounting procedure which compares timber management costs directly with receipts. It will be difficult to implement because the Forest Service budget does not take this form, but if properly developed, it may provide strong intra-agency incentive for economic efficiency in timber production and, concurrently, better provide for certain environmental and recreational values.

# 6

# An Institutional Dinosaur with an Ace

During the 1800's settlers rapidly moved westward. Forests covered much of what became the most productive farmland in the world. They expeditiously cleared many of these forests for farms, roads, homesteads, and towns. Because timber was plentiful, and cleared land scarce, a land inventory adjustment was necessary before settlers could begin making a successful agrarian livelihood. In sum, forested land was converted to farm land.

Lumber producers who wanted to stay in business would log forests in one area and, rather than invest in reforestation and remain in the same location, would move to cheaper lumber supplies in untouched areas. At that time, to do otherwise would have substantially decreased the probability of economic survival because the value of timber was so low that it was not worth the cost of reforestation even discounting years of income foregone during timber regrowth. Given the huge inventory of timber, such behavior probably made sense from both a private and social perspective.

Unfortunately, many high social costs accompanied this behavior as the lumber companies left stripped forest lands, clogged streams, and abandoned lumber towns in their wake. Other industries generated similar negative externalities during this period of rapid economic growth. The government gradually imposed regulations to control many of these social costs, e.g., the Pure Food and Drug Act of 1906. The forestry industry was perhaps unique in that not only did the government impose regulations, but it also instituted a system of national forests to be managed by the government through the U.S. Forest Service.

The federal government now owns and manages twenty percent of

This paper is a shortened adaptation by Kay Blemker of a paper with the same title presented at the September 1978 Liberty Fund-C.P.E.N.R. Conference on the Environmental Costs of Bureaucratic Government. Barney Dowdle is the author of the original paper. He is a Professor of Forestry at the University of Washington, Seattle.

the nation's commercial forestland. National parks and wilderness areas are not included in this commercial forest category because they are not logged and are only used for recreation and other aesthetic purposes.

The Forest Service employs the sustained yield-even flow method of forest management to provide "perpetual timber crops" and promote "community stability." This stability prevents previous practices which abandoned many towns shortly after they were established.

Under the sustained yield-even flow management system, the Forest Service harvests and replants timber at the same rate over a designated area. Ideally, within this system the amount harvested annually equals the annual growth. Once an area reaches the "regulated" stage, the Service harvests this "annual allowable cut" at the age of "culmination of mean annual increment" to maximize annual growth over time. It is important to realize that timber grows more slowly as it ages. When trees reach a certain age they are "ripe" in the sense that they make adequate logs and that an additional year of growth will produce less than any previous year. It will not produce enough to justify the opportunity foregone on land which could be growing new timber. "The total forest area (in acres) divided by the harvest age determine the acreage harvested each year." These practices result in "maximum sustained yield."

Many public forests are years, even decades, from being "regulated" and contain many acres of over-ripe timber. Harvesting this timber requires access to the entire forest, hence public foresters attempt to bulldoze and build their way to the oldest timber stands often without adequate regard for economic and environmental costs. The forester's model leaves many financial costs unincorporated, hence the Forest Service experiences an average 500 million dollar annual budget deficit.

Forest access roads are a well known source of erosion and hence stream pollution. The cost of erosion control and protection of water supplies is not fully accounted in the forester's model.

If current timber harvest rates depend directly on timber growth rates, increasing the growth rate allows the harvest rate to increase also. This correlation is known as the "allowable cut effect" (ACE). Instead of treating acres independently, ACE advocates applying sustained yield-even flow to the entire timber resources under Forest Service management. Forest Service managers argue that if they can increase the investment rate by growing more timber, then they have "earned the right" to liquidate more investments by harvesting more timber.

They make the mistake, however, of counting revenues from mature timber harvests as profits from the new acres of growing timber stands. This error is logically analogous to the following case.

If an individual cashes a mature war bond and purchases a new savings bond which matures in ten years, the profits from the mature savings bond could not count as profits from the one that is not yet mature. Yet forest managers use this accounting technique to calculate unheard of "rates of return" at annuity rates on investments which will not mature for over sixty years!

Many managers put these incredulous "rates of return" in benefit-cost ratio form to justify budget increases to grow more timber, and therefore to harvest more timber. Industry lobbyists use these "rates of return" to get more timber now because structural reform of the present system may take years, while timber is presently in short supply.

Sustained yield-even flow attempts to maximize growth over time, so public foresters strive to harvest older stands of timber with negligible growth rates before they cut into newer timber. The oldest stands tend to be the most remote and of highest elevations. In many timber sales contracts, the Forest Service specifies that road construction must precede the removal of timber, thereby passing the budgetary procedure and exhausting current wealth from timber profits by perpetuating wasteful and inappropriate forestry practices.

Road construction through forests promotes soil erosion and degrades water quality by increasing siltation. Consequently, by furthering the maximum growth objectives as defined by ACE, the forest service creates greater environmental repercussions using an immeasurably more expensive and inefficient forestry practice than the less costly and less environmentally damaging concentrated harvesting methods.

"Aesthetic logging" is another improvident practice by which topography determines logging site boundaries to ostensibly give a "natural" appearance, e.g., on ridges, valleys, rock slides, etc. Logging costs are very steep in these "natural" areas, and there is no evidence of increased environmental benefits which might justify the ensuing reduction in timber profits due to these increased costs.

Forest Service officials assert that the general populace desires all of these costly "benefits," therefore they have an obligation to provide them. Pressures to provide these "benefits" are indeed coming from somewhere, but the general public rarely even knows about these practices, and is therefore hardly in a position to advocate them! Public involvement with these issues consistently involves the same groups, i.e.,

51

bureaucrats and timber operators that will benefit from the prolongation of environmentally degrading and economically wasteful forestry management.

The Forest Service's ambiguous mandate permits it to justify almost any use of National Forests and escape cost accountability in the name of the "Multiple Use—Sustained Yield Act of 1964." The public taxpayer finances this squandering of public timber wealth through decreased profits received for timber because of high production costs and through an annual deficit now in the vicinity of 500 million dollars with expected incremental increases in the future.

If continued, present Forest Service management practices will create an "anemic" forest products industry. Although only twenty percent of the nation's commercial forestland is publicly owned, the federal government owns fifty percent of the national softwood sawtimber *inventory*. Softwood sawtimber provides the primary raw materials base for the lumber, plywood and pulp industries. In the West, where national forests are concentrated, the percentage of federally owned softwood sawtimber inventories is much higher. In Idaho, Oregon, and Washington, for example, the federal government owns over seventy percent of the softwood sawtimber reserves.

Until recently private timber stands have provided most of the raw materials for the forest products industry. Most of these resources were overmature virgin timber stands, and the owners liquidated these stands either to plant new stands or to convert the land to a higher valued use. The timber industry's demand for public timber has been steadily increasing because the second-crop private timber stands are not yet mature. Speculators, who previously counted on current overmature public timber supplies while private stands were regenerating, did not foresee the simultaneous increasing demand for recreational and environmental benefits. Consequently, timber supplies are much less than expected, and the processing industry has had to close mills and cut back production considerably.

Environmentalists accuse the industry of having cut all of its own timber and now wanting to dig into the public supply. They ignore the fact that the timber will inevitably be harvested in sequence, "private and then public old growth, followed by private and then public second growth, etc." (unless, of course, we all stop building wooden houses and furniture, paneling houses, using paper products, etc., for about 40 years).

The "even flow" concept in sustained yield-even flow policy is another aspect of public forestry management that is detrimental to the timber industry and ultimately to the consumers. The "even flow" timber sales policy generates instability in the industry by requiring small, short-term harvesting contracts. Price fluctuations in the timber industry make it more profitable to harvest timber when the price is "right." If the operators do not harvest public timber before their contract expires, however, they must pay the "difference between what they bid and the resale price of the timber."

The small sales make it infeasible for any individual operator to invest in the kinds of mills that would efficiently process the large virgin timber from public forests. Therefore, many timber processors are investing in small mills, which efficiently process second-growth private timber. What results is a public timber policy that, while bulldozing roads through forests to get at the largest, oldest timber in the most expensive manner, simultaneously discourages investment in mills that most efficiently process this timber. Thus the price of this timber rises again because more expensive processing is required.

"While the Forest Service and its supporters are quick to note that the national forests produce many non-marketed benefits, this does not preclude the fact that if they were being managed by economically rational criteria, society could have more wood and no less non-marketed forest benefits, more non-marketed forest benefits and no less wood, or more of both. More timber could be cut, but it would be cut in different locations such that conflicts between timber harvesting and the production of environmental amenities would be reduced."

## BIBLIOGRAPHY

Clawson, Marion. 1976. "The National Forests." *Science* 191:762-767.
Cong. Record, U.S. Senate. 1970. "A University View of the Forest Service" (The Bolle Reprt.) Cong. Record, Vol. 116, No. 84, Nov. 18, pp. S13401-S18408.
Davis, Kenneth P. *Forest Management*. McGraw-Hill, Inc., 1966.
Dowdle, Barney. "Perspectives on the Timber Supply Situation." Inst. of Gov. Res., Univ. of Wash., Wash. Public Policy Note Vol. 4, No. 2 (Spring 1976) 6 pp.
Forest Service. "Price Trends for Forest Products." U.S.D.A. Bull. 1956.
_____ 1970. Management Practices on the Bitterroot National Forest. A Task Force Analysis. Rpt. of Joint Northern Region-Intermtn. Sta. Task Force. 100 pp.
Hennes, LeRoy C., Michael J. Irving, and Daniel I. Navon. 1971. "Forest Control and Regulation: A Comparison of Traditional Methods and Alternatives." U.S.D.A., For. Ser., Res. Note PSW-231. 10 pp.
Levy, Yvonne. 1978. An Economic Alternative to Current Public Forest Policy. Reprint from Econ. Rev., Fed. Res. Bank of San Francisco (Wtr. edition) 22 pp.
Schweitzer, Dennis L., Robert W. Sassaman, and Con H. Schallan. "Allowable Cut Effect: Some Physical and Economic Implications." *Journal of Forestry* (1972):415-418.
Waggener, Thomas R. 1969. "Some Economic Implications of Sustained Yield as a Forest Regulation Model." Inst. of For. Prod., Univ. of Wash. Cont. For. Paper, Contribution No. 6. 22 pp.

# 7

## Dams and Other Disasters: The Social Costs of Federal Water Development Policies

In 1824, the Supreme Court ruled that the federal government has the power to regulate interstate commerce, including navigation on rivers and harbors. This decree enabled the government to benefit trade by developing canals and removing snags, rocks, and sandbars that interfered with barge and steamboat traffic. Initially, the government assigned the U.S. Army Corps of Engineers to keep waterways navigable. By the end of the 19th century, successive legislation gave this Defense Department agency responsibility over bridges, wharves, piers, channels, harbors, water diversion, and refuse disposal—functions far removed from national defense.

The 1902 Reclamation Act established the Bureau of Reclamation as a self-supporting agency to loan money for irrigation projects in the arid western states and to collect fees and interest from the sale of water to cover construction costs. The Bureau soon expanded its mission to include power, flood control, recreation, and fisheries, simultaneously abandoning its self-supporting budget and charging the federal government with a segment of the non-irrigation benefits.

Numerous other water development projects such as the Tennessee Valley Authority (TVA) and the Soil Conservation Service (SCS) were created to provide useful services and, after fulfilling the need for those services, they developed into powerful bureaucracies with self-imposed duties that are often environmentally degrading and economically infeasible. President Roosevelt created the TVA during the depression to

This paper is a shortened adaptation by Kay Blemker of a paper entitled, "Dams and Disasters: The Social Problems of Federal Water Development Policies," which was presented at the September 1978 Liberty Fund-C.P.E.N.R. Conference on the Environmental Costs of Bureaucratic Government. Bernard Shanks is the author of the original paper. In addition to being Associate Professor of Forestry and Outdoor Recreation at Utah State University, Shanks is a member of the Executive Council of the Wilderness Society.

provide jobs in the Appalachian Mountains through a unique regional development corporation with comprehensive responsibility for both water and related land resources. The Soil Conservation Service in the Department of Agriculture was initially responsible for alleviating the problems of the Kansas dust bowl and insuring that similar consequences did not occur from unwise farming practices elsewhere in the West. In 1954, Public Law 566 gave the SCS responsibility for watershed projects and dams with less than 25,000 acre feet of capacity. It provided technical assistance and loans to private parties for smaller dam projects.

In the Spring of 1943, the Missouri River flooded adjoining lands to heights not reached since 1881, causing fifty million dollars in damages. Congress reacted by requesting a review of the flood control "needs" of the Missouri from the Corps of Engineers. Referring to their 1,245 page Missouri River Report completed in 1934, the Corps came up with the "Pick Plan." This short (12-page) report was a flood control and navigation plan for the lower Missouri Basin that included levees, five large main stem dams and six dams on major tributaries.

The Pick Plan ignored upstream irrigation interests, but the Bureau of Reclamation had spent five years in developing the "Sloan Plan." This plan stressed irrigation, but also included flood control and navigation on the lower Missouri. It was much more detailed and comprehensive than the Pick Plan, proposing 90 reservoirs, facilities to irrigate 4.7 million acres of land, and projects to produce 4 billion kilowatts of water generated power.

Both agencies fought for their own plans and criticized the other. Newspapers and Congressmen supported whichever agency benefitted their primary clientele and constituencies. Controversy over the two plans heightened until September 21, 1944, when President Roosevelt asked Congress to create a Missouri Valley Authority (MVA), patterned after the Tennessee Valley Authority. Unable to control his two major water agencies, President Roosevelt proposed a new agency.

On October 16 and 17, representatives of the Corps and Bureau met in Omaha and reached a one-page agreement known as the "Pick-Sloan" plan. In two days, these two agencies decided the *entire* development plan for the largest river in North America without any outside involvement and in opposition to a Presidential proposal. This union between two ancient adversaries put an end to the Missouri Valley Authority and saved the special interest clientele of both groups.

Unable to agree on the best projects, the Corps and the Bureau decided to build almost everything. Each agency reconciled itself to the works of the other; however, the Pick-Sloan plan did eliminate one Pick project because the site would have been submerged by a larger Sloan project downstream.

The Bureau's Regional Director had testified earlier that the Garrison Dam site was not only wasteful but dangerous. Yet he approved the project in the Pick-Sloan compromise. The Pick-Sloan Plan ignored such important basic considerations as allocation of water to navigation, flood control, power, land use, and regional distribution of benefits. Navigation had won the lower basin, irrigation the upper basin, and no one knew if enough water existed for both.

Congress provided six billion dollars, and the two agencies constructed dams for over thirty years. However, no agency examined the effectiveness of the two-day plan or even asked if it was achieving its objectives. One thing is certain—nowhere in the history of water policy were so many dams approved in such a short time by so few people.

Water projects were the first to have a specific economic test required during planning; the use of cost-benefit analysis grew out of Section 1 of the Flood Control Act of 1936 (47 Stat. 1570). Congress stated that "the Federal Government should improve or participate in the improvement of navigable waters or their tributaries, including watersheds thereof for flood control purposes if the benefits to whomsoever they may accrue are in excess of the estimated costs."

Within a few years, cost-benefit analysis was used to justify all federal water development projects. However, early analyses failed to take intangible benefits into account because intangibles are not readily quantifiable. Tangible benefits and costs are of two types—direct and indirect. Decisions about indirect or secondary benefits and costs allow for much flexibility which requires the use of subjective judgment. Secondary benefits are often enhanced and the secondary costs, particularly in human or social terms, are underestimated.

Originally, federal water projects were limited to navigation, but, as waterborne transportation shrank, flood control became the primary justification for federal involvement in water development. The rise in multiple purpose water projects complicated and duplicated the roles of federal water development agencies. Agencies are now involved in power production, transmission facilities, water quality concerns, recreation, domestic and industrial water supplies, and even weather modification. Although they may not be cost effective, federal water projects undoubtedly provide some benefit to both public and private parties. It is the *allocation* of costs and benefits to both parties that has been increasingly complex and controversial. Who receives the benefits and who pays the costs of public water projects? We will examine this question as it applied to our own case study of the Pick-Sloan Plan and to water projects in general.

Many problems resulted from federal water developments. Dams were forced to sites unsuited for private development. The public developments grew larger and larger because agencies could minimize design costs by using the same design in more than one location, regardless of the location's specific characteristics. Western states lost some of the best agriculture, wildlife, waterfowl, and other natural resource sites that were located along the banks of the major rivers. The ranching economy was often tied to river bottomland, which was often critical for livestock operations.

When federal water development agencies were planning and constructing between the 1930's and 1950's, massive technological improvements occurred in transferring power long distances. Instead of reversing the migration from rural to urban areas as promised, many projects augmented the population flow to urban areas by supplying power, hence industries and jobs, to the cities.

After the initial construction phase, many rural areas were left without any new businesses, a loss of superior agriculture lands, and part of the tax base to the reservoir. The projects disrupted traditional patterns of transportation, communication, and economic activity, and the seasonal influxes of recreationalists proved difficult and expensive to manage. The cost-benefit analyses neglected to consider the *geographic* distribution of costs and benefits. Benefits flowed to the city, while costs often stayed close to the development site.

Decades after the completion of the Pick-Sloan Plan, studies found that it had failed to attract industries to non-industrial areas, reverse out-migration from rural areas, reduce the percentages of people on welfare, or lower the cost of public services. Further, in spite of the justification, *this plan did not even reduce flood damages.*

The Pick-Sloan plan did replace the subsistence economy of the Missouri Indians with a welfare economy. Indian reservations were cheap to acquire; urban areas were expensive. A positive cost-benefit ratio was enhanced by flooding the reservation and protecting the city. The analysis conveniently neglected to consider the devastating effect of the project on a culture that had remained largely intact for thousands of years. River bottomland provided quality cropland not found elsewhere on the upland plains, habitat for game animals, pasture for domestic stock, and timber for heat, buildings, and shelter. The Garrison Dam construction disrupted the entire social, economic, and cultural life of the tribes involved. One-thousand-seven-hundred people lost their homes, burial grounds and religious sites. They also lost ninety percent of their timber and much of the wildlife habitat. Furthermore, after bearing a disproportionate share of the costs, the Indians did not share the development benefits. The only cost that the Army Corps of Engineers considered in its analysis was the reservation land, acquired at less than $100 per acre.

The Pick-Sloan projects, so quickly authorized, may not only be inefficient but may be one of the least optimal methods of utilizing Missouri River resources. Although such projects have a fixed life span, the Army Corps of Engineers and other water development agencies disregard the economic life span and exclude programs to update the projects. These agencies also fail to evaluate and plan the eventual redevelopment or undevelopment of such programs in almost all of their analyses.

Many water development projects cost-benefit analyses neglect to consider problems over time. Construction errors and other factors often require the modification and rebuilding of many projects, which often cost more than the initial construction. Analysts can cut their estimates to less than half of the actual required budget by ignoring these maintenance and rehabilitation costs.

Safety is another neglected problem that is related to time. Dam safety decreases with age. Because of numerous recent dam failures, insurance companies have been refusing to insure private dams. Proposed legislation would federally guarantee liability insurance for private water projects. This would not only encourage dam construction through a subsidy, but also discourage safety programs, rehabilitation, and responsible management behavior by the dam owner.

Federal water development projects have traded predictable and low risk flooding for unpredictable risk with very high costs. The Teton Dam failure caused a massive man-made flood with damages exceeding one billion dollars, although the estimated benefits of the project were only a few million dollars. As the Fort Peck Dam ages, the likelihood of failure increases. The initial cost-benefit analysis did not include the costs of a dam failure in the rationale for federal construction. If the benefits of avoiding low level predictable floods are included, the costs of a massive man-made flood should also be included in this analysis.

The U.S. Water Resources Council has recently added more detailed evaluation to the social and non-economic aspects of water resource planning. Yet, because of a lack of experience and a lack of basic data upon which to base analysis, analysts still disagree on which methodology of benefit-cost accounting to use.

Furthermore, Congress has authorized many projects over the past thirty years that have not yet been funded. Ignoring economic efficiency and new social concerns, Congress continues or initiates these projects as funds become available. The constituents that benefit from the federal development agencies and the federal tax money are specific and have a clear and readily understandable interest in continuing the existing system. The rural to urban flow of resources, economic power, and political influence serves to widen the disparity in geographic distribution of benefits, leaving the rural residents much worse, both socially and economically, than before federal agencies built water projects in their area. Consultants, engineering firms, and construction companies have a concise understanding of the committee process and appreciate the agencies that propose the projects and the politicians that deliver the appropriations. Government bureaucrats have a tenacity and dedication to their goals that pales all but the most zealous environmentalist.

Actual improvements in federal water development policy will require institutional reform. Separating the cost-benefit analysis from the agency involved and assigning the analysis to an independent group, such as the Office of Management and Budget, would eliminate much of the discretion that the agency now has in deciding the size and scope of its own programs. This reform would result in a more detailed and comprehensive account of those who receive benefits and those who would pay the economic, social, and cultural costs. A visual geographical demonstration of the distribution of benefits and costs would vividly illustrate the inequities which are almost always ignored or made light of in agency evaluations.

Reform measures should also include a complete evaluation of costs and benefits over time, with updated data bases and continual re-evaluation to determine optimal use of water resources. Advance planning and preparation of project dismantling or re-development would prevent many of the unforeseen negative effects that accompany these types of changes. Reforms to fund minority advocates with grants, included in the development costs, for mitigation and exploration of alternatives would help present a complete and comprehensive display of costs and benefits for decision-makers in the political process.

All of these reform measures will allow for the opportunity to correct past mistakes and write off sunken costs. A continual monitoring for efficiency and planned re-development would be an improvement on the present situation. If nothing else, more people would be drawn into the "cozy relationship" the water triumvirate now enjoys.

## BIBLIOGRAPHY

Shanks, Bernard. "The American Indian and Missouri River Water Developments." ment." *Water Resources Bulletin*, Vol. 13, No. 2. April 1977. pp. 255-263.

Shanks, Bernard. "The American Indian and Missouri River Water Developments." *Water Resources Bulletin*. Vol. IV, No. 3. June 1974. pp. 573-579.

The best summary of the Pick-Sloan issue is Marian E. Ridgeway's, "The Missouri Basin's Pick-Sloan Plan," Illinois Studies in the Social Science. Vol. 35. The University of Illinois Press. 1955.

Two of the few ex post evaluation studies found major errors in both the benefits and costs achieved at large project. See Haveman, Robert H. *The Economic Performance of Public Investments*. The John Hopkins Press. 1972. and Shanks, Bernard D. *Indicators of Missouri River Project Effects on Local Residents: An Advocacy Resource Development Approach*. Unpublished Ph.D. Thesis, Michigan State University. 1974.

U.S. Dept. of Agriculture, Economic Research Service. "A History of Federal Water Resources Programs, 1800-1960." Misc. Publication No. 1233. Washington, D.C. June 1972. p. 3.

U.S. Senate, Committee on Environment and Public Works. "National Dam Inspection Act Amendments." 95th Cong. 2d Sess., Serial No. 95-H43. p. 001.

# 8

## Policy-Induced Demand for Coal Gasification

Coal gasification in the United States is unlikely to be economical for commercial purposes for the remainder of this century. However, regulatory distortions will probably cause us to buy commercial quantities of synthetic gas (SNG) made from coal within the next ten to fifteen years. This paper presents evidence supporting both of these hypotheses and explains the various perverse impacts of governmental pricing policies that, ironically enough, are intended to prevent economic inefficiencies and to benefit gas consumers.

Natural gas price regulations keep the market price of gas below what it would be in a free market. Gas shortages, caused by regulation, have intensified every symptom of the "energy crisis." Electricity blackouts are promoted by energy demands otherwise served by gas, which would be produced or not used by current consumers at higher gas prices. Oil import demands are similarly inflated, and domestic oil supplies are reduced to the extent that marginal wells are not exploited because companies cannot sell the gas associated with the oil at a market clearing price. Therefore, they simply burn off the marginal gas.

Sophisticated environmental groups are among those recognizing the tradeoff of environmental quality which will result from prematurely exploiting the vast energy potential of U.S. coal and oil shale. The Environmental Defense Fund (EDF) has been intervening in natural gas court cases to encourage the development of marginal cost pricing. This plan would require each user to pay the full system cost of his/her own gas consumption and receive the full benefit of conservation.

The high cost of SNG, whether measured by energy efficiency, water and environmental costs, or simply in dollar values, indicates strongly

This paper is a shortened adaptation by Kay Blemker of a paper with the same title presented at the September 1978 Liberty Fund-C.P.E.N.R. Conference on the Environmental Costs of Bureaucratic Government. Richard L. Stroup is the author of the original paper. He is also a Professor of Economics and Co-Director of the Center for Political Economy and Natural Resources at Montana State University.

that a socially efficient energy strategy would exclude commercial production of SNG for at least several decades. Nonetheless, federal energy strategy is rapidly moving toward subsidized production of SNG using commercially untried technologies.

The following sections will describe SNG, give a rationale for its production, and summarize with suggestions for alternative energy strategies.

The Lurgi process of combining crushed coal with steam and oxygen under high pressure is the most thoroughly proven method of producing SNG. However, the resulting mixture of hydrogen, hydrocarbons, nitrogen, and carbon oxides is unsuitable for pipeline-quality gas.

Pipeline-quality SNG requires the commercially unproven process of methanation, which removes all carbon monoxide and some carbon dioxide while raising the heating value to 900-1,000 British thermal units per standard cubic foot (Btu/scf). Although scientists are exploring newer technologies, the first plants are expected to use the Lurgi process with methanation.[1]

SNG handles easily and burns cleanly, so it is less environmentally objectionable than many other alternative fuels, including the coal from which it is made. SNG *production* is an entirely different matter. It seems fairly obvious that environmental and health dangers would result from a number of harmful chemicals discharged into effluent streams, product streams, and the surrounding atmosphere from any future SNG plant.[2]

The current shortage of natural gas carries the most weight towards plans to produce SNG from coal in the near future because SNG is a direct substitute for gas, though it often has slightly less energy content per unit volume. The present gas shortage began in 1971, but its cause dates back to the 1950's when the Federal Power Commission began regulating natural gas wellhead prices. The Federal Power Commission (now the Federal Energy Regulatory Commission) controls its prices below a market clearing level (where the amount produced equals the amount demanded by consumers). Until as recently as 1970, new wellhead prices were below $.20 per thousand cubic feet (MCF). Electricity costs at the plant were at least ten times greater at that time. Even today, interstate gas wellhead prices are less than one third the cost of electricity at new plants.

[1]Office of Coal Research, U.S. Department of the Interior, "Evaluation of Coal Gasification Technology, Part I: Pipeline Quality Gas" (Washington, D.C.: Government Printing Office, 1973).
[2]Stanley M. Greenfield, "Environmental Problems with Fossil Fuels," *Options for U.S. Energy Policy,* Institute for Contemporary Studies, 1977.

Gas is a clean and continuously deliverable fuel source which makes it very valuable, especially to home consumers. The value of gas is understated with controlled prices. Consumers not only demand more than if higher market prices prevailed, but the *structure* of regulated rates further increases the demand through declining block rates, where *extra* gas use is priced below the customer's average cost. Controlled prices also retard incentives to search for and produce gas from untapped sources.

Since SNG supplements will cost close to $5.00 per MCF, distributors will probably "roll-in" SNG with cheaper natural gas. Consumers of the new gas will then pay only about half of its cost, and a higher price for all natural gas in the system will capture the other half. Currently, the federally regulated ceiling price on domestic gas sold in interstate markets is $1.50 per MCF. A distributor buying eighty percent of its gas at $1.40 per MCF and twenty percent SNG at $5.50 per MCF would show an average cost of $2.22 per MCF. If the distributor placed distribution costs on the first few MCFs purchased per month by each customer, most people would face an average gas cost of $2.22 per MCF on the marginal gas purchased or saved. Hence, the importance of rolled-in pricing to the success of SNG sales becomes apparent.

The declining block rate structure allows the customer who uses an extra MCF of gas to pay only half the cost. This consumer can purchase gas at an average cost of $2.22 per MCF that costs the distributor (and therefore its customers as a group) $5.50 per MCF. Customers who normally use a smaller amount of gas or conserve on gas use are penalized by paying higher gas prices and are, in effect, subsidizing those who use greater amounts of gas.

The combination of Federal wellhead regulation and state distributor regulation means that expensive SNG becomes partially a common pool resource and high cost is not the deterrent to SNG production that efficiency would demand. Only in this sort of price-distorted environment would a firm seeking profits want to invest a billion dollars to produce a product not expected to cover its cost of production. Yet this cross subsidy of SNG by natural gas users is being proposed at this writing.

Rate-of-return regulations distort the regulated firm's view of production cost vs. delivery uncertainties. With a regulated rate-of-return, a firm will presumably avoid risky ventures, even if the expected rate-of-return exceeds both normal and regulated rates. If the venture fails, the firm will bear most of the costs, while if the project should be a big winner, the firm could not collect the profits.

Small gambles might be acceptable, however, at least on the production cost side. Utilities could cover a fifty percent overrun on plant costs for a SNG project by raising the regulated rolled-in price of the natural gas enough to cover the extra cost (assuming the firm's gas demand to be sufficiently inelastic in the regulated context).

Small gambles on the output side might be unacceptable to the firm because a utility which cannot deliver part of its planned output will probably not be paid for that output. Forcing other customers to pay extra for fixed costs, plus an allowed return on distribution capacity built to serve customers cut off in a shortage, may not be acceptable to the regulating agency. Therefore, the utility itself may be forced to bear the costs from this type of loss. Even if consumers can switch temporarily or permanently to coal or oil, this socially minor risk becomes large as viewed by the gas utility.

This distorted view of risk plus federal subsidies for SNG process development efforts and proposed loan guarantees for commercial plants cause gas distributors to encourage SNG production efforts. The firm has distorted incentives and the regulatory commission may well be less than perfectly informed and/or perfectly unbiased.

Pipeline-quality synthetic gas production is not a commercially proven technology. Researchers must conduct extensive research and development before the first plant operates, and the funding is not yet available. Significant amounts of development are required in high-pressure feed systems, pollutant analysis and control, application of technology to various coal types, the methanation process, and scaling-up processes from experimental to commercial size. Engineering problems of actual plant construction, such as field erection and fabrication of pressure cheaper than SNG, need much work before commercial production can begin. The SNG processes, inefficient in terms of economics, thermodynamics, and the environment, simply could not stand careful scrutiny were it not for the direct and indirect governmental interference mentioned above.

It is ironic that collective action taken presumably to correct failures in a purely volunteer, or market setting now are seen to cause serious inefficiencies in the sense that resources with high replacement costs are used as if they were cheap. Inequities result from such action as a user can use more and shift much of the cost to others. Increased environmental burdens also result since more oil and coal are used in place of cleaner, but wasted and undiscovered gas. The most direct way to attack these problems would be, of course, to eliminate the collective actions causing them and to rely on voluntary exchange. Another approach would be to change public policies to try and mimic the market and thus keep regulation in place.

A return to the free market in natural gas at the wellhead would result in higher natural gas prices, no gas shortage, and reduced demand for oil and coal. Such a system would also eliminate the demand for SNG from coal. Owners of residential gas hookups would be affected by the higher burner tip gas price. Energy users forced to use oil, coal, or a similarly expensive energy form due to gas shortages (or for other reasons) would be better off without wellhead gas price regulation since demand, new production, and prices of those energy alternatives would fall. Public policy makers should probably be reminded that "profit" is not a four letter word and free exchange is normally a positive sum game.

Federal subsidies to SNG commercialization would have to be stopped by political means. Since there are no apparent positive technological externalities to SNG production, the argument for subsidies is strictly redistributive. Although higher wellhead natural gas prices are a far cheaper way to get more gas to consumers, the common pool resource known as the federal treasury is a tempting target for those whose jobs, establishment profits, or regional development depend on federal money.

Eliminating rolled-in pricing and declining block rates would undoubtedly improve regulation, but total utility bills would still fail to reflect the total opportunity cost to serve a given customer.

It is useful to note in closing that any reduction in private property rights is likely to be costly, whether by price regulation or other means. Either the incentive to produce for the benefit of others is reduced, or the incentive to conserve resources is reduced. Often both results occur. Further, since individual responsibility is at least partly curtailed, individual authority to act (freedom) must also be limited. Unconstrained private rights are of course demonstrably imperfect in predictable circumstances. Monopoly, externality, and public goods problems all argue for the consideration of collective action. The result of collective actions on SNG production probabilities, however, indicates strongly that "corrective" collective action can create far worse problems than the problem it attempts to solve. Although "protected" from paying higher prices to gas well owners and higher profits to distributors, gas users (and potential users) face both shortages *and* the likelihood of being required to pay for high cost SNG.

# BIBLIOGRAPHY

Boulanger, R. E., "Additional Prepared Testimony," July 14, 1978, before Federal Energy Regulatory Commission, Docket Nos. CP78-391, CP75-278, CP77-556.

Breyer, S. G. and P. W. MacAvoy, *Energy Regulation by the Federal Power Commission,* Washington, DC: The Brookings Institution, 1974.

Garvey, J. R., et. al., *Final Report of the Supply-Technical Advisory Task Force— Synthetic Gas-Coal* (Washington, DC: FPC, April 1973).

Greenfield, Stanley M., "Environmental Problems with Fossil Fuels" in *Options for U.S. Energy Policy,* San Francisco: Institute for Contemporary Studies, 1977.

Hammond, O. and M. Zimmerman, "The Economics of Coal-Based Synthetic Gas," *Technology Review* (M.I.T., Cambridge, July–August 1975).

Mause, P. J. and J. H. Bailey, "Brief of the Environmental Defense Fund, Before the Public Service Commission of Wisconsin," 6680-GR-3, February 6, 1978.

Office of Coal Research, U.S. Department of the Interior, "Evaluation of Coal Gasification Technology, Part I: Pipeline Quality Gas" (Washington, DC: Government Printing Office, 1973).

Pindyck, Robert S., "Prices and Shortages: Policy Options for the National Gas Industry" in *Options for U.S. Energy Policy,* San Francisco: Institute for Contemporary Studies, 1977.

Stroup, R. L. and V. House, "The Political Economy of Coal Gasification: Some Determinants of Demand for Western Coal," (Staff Paper 75-17, Department of Agricultural Economics and Economics, Montana State University, 1975).

Stroup, R. L. and W. N. Thurman, "Will Coal Gasification Come to the Northern Great Plains?" *Montana Business Quarterly,* Winter 1976.

# Part Three

# 9

# Property Rights, Cowboys and Bureaucrats: A Modest Proposal

Concern with reforming government can be expressed in several constructive forms. Each, of course, should be evaluated in terms of its relative impact on projected social welfare. Examples of reforms include limits on spending, private delivery of public services and economic impact evaluations of government regulations. In addition to the above strategies there is also a potential for converting public to private assets. Opportunities in this area abound in the field of natural resources. Obvious examples include forest and range lands in the West.

Although the focus of such discussions is usually upon relatively narrowly defined economic efficiency, i.e., entries on a conventional balance sheet, this paper stresses the *environmental* benefits reasonably expected to result from one such reform. In this, as in similar opportunities for improvement, it is difficult to estimate whether the financial or the environmental improvements will dominate.

The Bureau of Land Management in the U.S. Department of Interior administers 171 million acres of public land in eleven western states. This acreage exceeds that of Utah, Wyoming and Idaho. Most of this land is arid and has predominantly been used for grazing. Until 1964 the major legal objective for the BLM was to administer grazing privileges on public lands. This scope was broadened in 1964 and the Federal Land Policy and Management Act of 1976, Section 202 of the BLM "Organic Act," requires the BLM to manage in accord with principles of multiple use and sustained yield.

For most of our history the dominant federal land policy has been to sell or grant public lands to the states, individuals, or businesses. The purpose of this policy was to generate revenue from sales, aid settle-

The descriptive section of this paper draws heavily from two papers presented at the L.F.-CPENR Conference. They are S. Kremp, "A Perspective on BLM's Proposed Grazing Policy," and Ron Lanner, "Chained to the Bottom."

ment, and provide an economic base for citizens. The Congresses of the early and middle 19th century did not expect one third of the nation to remain in federal ownership.

During the period of disposal, a very large portion of the marginally productive western land was practically ignored. Because the productivity of the land was so low and the various Homestead Acts so restrictive this land was not patented. It was, however, grazed as a huge common property pasture. By 1850 cattle and sheepmen utilized significant portions of this free forage. It is very important to understand that no property rights to this land were legally defined. Therefore, the benefit of adding animals to the range was received by the individual stockman while the cost was dispersed among all users. In this common property situation if the benefits of the stockman of adding one cow or sheep outweighed *his* costs, then additional animals will continue to be added. Thus, serious overgrazing resulted. This is the classic "tragedy of the commons."

As a result of the above process the productivity of the public range was greatly reduced by 1900. Heavy overgrazing led to range deterioration and erosion. By the 1930's the ranchers recognized that investments in institutional reform would be productive.

Obviously, transfers of grazing lands to private ownerships would have improved the situation dramatically. Under private ownership there would be strong incentives to stock the range at optimal rates. The benefits and costs of adding livestock and of intensifying management would both be faced by the operator. With private ownership, a rancher and his heirs would suffer the losses resulting from reduced value and productivity.

The alternative plan which was adopted established a governmental agency to regulate the use of the public range lands. In June of 1934 the Taylor Grazing Act established the Grazing Service in the Department of Interior. Although the Act probably improved upon the unregulated commons, it did not provide a solution to the problems. Both equity and efficiency violations were highly visible. As a result of general dissatisfaction with management the Grazing Service and the General Land Office were consolidated into the Bureau of Land Management in 1946.

## Problems with Current Management

The two basic sources of dissatisfaction with the current management of BLM's grazing lands are a lack of environmental sensitivity and a failure to consider economic efficiency. These deficiencies are considered below.

According to BLM's own assessment only seventeen percent of the range land administered by BLM is in good or excellent condition.[1] Although the conditions have improved somewhat over the past forty years, the BLM range is not in as good condition as adjoining private land and National Forest range lands.[2] Further, the agency acknowledges that its land is *not* properly managed; conditions are declining and are expected to continue to decline under the present system.[3]

It is obvious that improvements are in order. Yet two management strategies adopted by the BLM, "rest rotation grazing" and "chaining," have a very high potential of further *reducing* environmental quality.

**Rest Rotation**

Rest rotation is a grazing system whose best feature appears to be its name. Most simply, a grazing allotment is fenced into three or four pastures. The first section is intensively grazed during the entire period, the second is grazed after forage grasses have gone to seed, and the third is rested. By keeping the same amount of stock on the allotment as prior to the fencing, livestock will be forced to consume nearly all vegetation. Thus a pasture in rest rotation may be stocked two or three times as densely as under continuous grazing. Although one can under-

---

[1] BLM, 1975 b., *Range Condition Report, National Resource Lands,* Colorado, Mimeo.
[2] The reason why we might expect private land to be in better shape than BLM lands was touched upon earlier. First of all, many private ranches were never overgrazed as badly as the public range since they were not initially a part of the commons situation. Secondly, ranchers benefit directly from maintaining their land in a healthy, productive state. BLM officials tend to benefit from the political support of their constituents. Due to strong pressures from livestock interests, they have not raised forage fees to market value, and they have not always lowered the number of permitted cattle and sheep within the carrying capacity of the range. The range users, who do not own the range and who are not certain that they will be able to continue using the range, also have no real incentive to conserve range quality. So, in a sense, the tragedy of the commons continues on BLM land.

Forest Service range land faces some of the same problems as BLM range, and much of it is also overgrazed. However, the Forest Service began managing its range land in 1905, twenty-nine years earlier than the Grazing Service. Much of the land now administered by the Forest Service was never in as bad condition and has had a long time to recover than the land administered by the BLM. In addition, Forest Service land is usually at a higher elevation and wetter than BLM land and thus recovers more quickly from abuse. From Sabine C. Kremp, "A Perspective on BLM's Proposed Grazing Policy," in a volume on Natural Resource Economic Policy forthcoming from The University of Michigan Press.
[3] BLM, 1975 a., *Range Condition Report Prepared for the Senate Committee on Appropriations.* U.S. Department of Interior. U.S. Govt. Printing Office.

stand the situation of BLM bureaucrats—clearly they face strong incentives to do something—it is not at all clear that rest rotation will even fulfill the single object of increasing the forage available.

Forage production, however, is only one aspect of environmental quality. Watershed protection is also important and is likely to suffer as a result of this practice. Cattle crowded into a pasture increase soil compaction and thus decrease water infiltration. It is indeed likely that sheet erosion would result from a high intensity storm hitting a pasture recently subjected to intensive grazing.

Wildlife is an important resource on BLM range lands. Fencing restricts the movement of big game animals and results in increased mortality. Further, if the program works, shrubs are largely replaced by grasses. Thus, deer, sage grouse and other species dependent on shrubs may be severely affected by the elimination of sage and little brush. Glen Griffith, Director of the Nevada Fish and Game Department, expressed his concern in a letter to the Nevada BLM which stated "...there is no alternative for the Nevada Fish and Game Department except to heartily condemn the (grazing) proposal as being detrimental to wildlife and not meeting the test of the "Organic Act" definition of land management for multiple uses."

The existence of riparion vegetation is critical to fish habitat. These plants provide benefits to fish and aquatic insects by providing hiding places, reducing stream erosion by retarding current velocities, and mechanically holding soil particles. Even the most casual observation indicated that intensive grazing on stream banks has detrimental impacts upon this vegetation. In sum, the relatively capital intensive practice of rest rotation grazing produces significant environmental costs.

**Chaining**

Chaining is a spectacular management technique. This process involves clearing pinyon and juniper woodlands by connecting two D8 size crawler tractors with 600 feet of anchor chain and dragging the chain through the stand of trees. Debris may be left in place or piled into windrows. The area is then seeded with grasses, especially crested wheatgrass of Central Asian origin. Most chaining has been done in Arizona, New Mexico, Utah, and Nevada. The total area chained in these states reached about three million acres by 1964. Between 1960 and 1972 the BLM chained in excess of 250,000 acres in Utah alone.[4]

---

[4]Ronald Lanner, "Chained to the Bottom," in a volume on Natural Resource Economic Policy, University of Michigan Press, forthcoming.

Since the development of the environmental movement it has been rather difficult to obtain data on this practice. Neither the BLM in the Department of Interior nor the Forest Service in the Department of Agriculture publicized their chaining programs until NEPA mandated the preparation of environmental impact statements. The Forest Service complied by preparing nearly identical statements for Utah and Nevada but the BLM did not appear to have such statements by November of 1978.

The rationale for chaining is plant control. The presumption is that trees have been invading grasslands and greedily displacing grasses and other forage. This view offers the agencies a sense of mission. As Lanner notes: "There is even an aura of melodrama, with the private rancher as victim, the woodlands as villian, and the agency the hero with a bulldozer on each hip." While this perspective is highly convenient for the bureaucratic entrepreneur, the invasion hypothesis remains undemonstrated and is open to fundamental doubt. Regardless of the validity of the hypothesis, chaining does provide a secure budgeting item; it builds support for the agencies among the stockmen clientele, and provides inducements when dealing with stockmen who might otherwise be uncooperative. Unfortunately, there is good evidence that the practice is environmentally destructive and economically inefficient. In brief, if as a matter of policy, we are to subsidize small portions of the livestock industry, we would do well to merely send federal checks and forget about wasting the diesel fuel and tearing up the landscape.

Although chaining does in fact increase forage production, the relevant policy questions are what are the benefits and what are the opportunity costs of this action. Again, there are at least two types of benefits that are relevant. The first is environmental and the second is financial.

Research indicates that, despite agency claims to the contrary, there are no watershed benefits associated with chaining. Likewise, although the practice is particularly justified in terms of wildlife welfare, no such benefits have been established as resulting from the practice of chaining.[5] Deer in particular are reluctant to expose themselves in expansive chained areas, many of which are hundreds or thousands of acres in size.

While chaining may have no benefits aside from increments in forage production it clearly has several negative impacts in addition to the vis-

[5]Terrel, Ted. L., and J. Spillett. 1975. "Pinyon-juniper conversion: its impact on mule deer and other wildlife." In The pinyon-juniper ecosystem: a symposium, pp. 105-119. Utah State Univ. Coll. Nat. Res. and Utah Agric. Exp. Sta., Logan, Utah.

ual disturbances. According to a Forest Service archaeologist it may accomplish a 100 percent wipeout of archaeological sites. In addition, it deprives local Indians (Shoshone and Paiute) of important sources of winter food—the pine nut. Thus the traditional Indian winter food supply is decimated to accommodate a subsidy to white men's cattle. Fortunately, however, after generations of dependence upon the good intentions of federal bureaucracies the Indians should not be surprised at their treatment. Perhaps Deloria had a point when he suggested that the White could profitably learn from the Indian's experience.

### Financial Costs of Rest Rotation

Rest rotation requires substantial capital investments. Thousands of miles of fences must be constructed on what are often difficult circumstances. The cost of these "improvements" often run from $3,000 to $4,000 per mile as it takes a rather substantial fence to turn a hungry 1,100 pound cow or a hungry 1,600 bull. Further, each pasture must have a dependable water supply which often requires spring or well development and expensive piping. BLM has estimated that the cost of implementing this intensive range management program will be about $328.6 million and will carry an annual cost of $33.3 million.[6]

Costs, however, tell us little until compared with benefits. The primary beneficiaries of this practice are officials of the BLM and perhaps some livestock operators. Many ranchers are skeptical.

Fourteen range allotments were analyzed in a Nevada study. An optimistically projected increase in forage production was expected to increase the yield of grazing fees over the fifteen year planning period. A comparison of costs of implementing the systems to the returns showed:

> The internal rate of return was computed for eleven of the fourteen observations (allotments). Three observations had to be deleted because net returns for each year over the entire planning horizon were negative. The magnitude of the internal rate of return on the remaining eleven observations ranged from −0.18 to 0.42. The mean was 0.01.[7]

In sum, on average it would have made financial sense to adopt rest rotation management *only* if money could be borrowed at less than one percent interest. Even this makes optimistic assumptions regarding productivity and disregards environmental costs. In this case we again

---

[6]BLM, 1975 a. *Range Condition Report Prepared for the Senate Committee on Appropriations.* U.S. Department of Interior. U.S. Govt. Printing Office.
[7]Rozell, D. G., C. T. K. Ching and C. E. Hancock, 1973. *Economic Returns of Rest Rotation Grazing to the Bureau of Land Management.* University of Nevada, Reno.

expect that the American tax payer will be subsidizing the deterioration of the public range lands.

## Financial Costs of Chaining

Although chaining has been practiced for decades benefit-cost analysis were not conducted until the mid-1970's. A 1975 study lead by a respected range economist produced a benefit-cost ratio of less than one, specifically 0.86 benefits to 1.00 costs.[8] We should also note that clearing costs nearly four times those used in the study have been reported. A government report indicated that under 1972 conditions, i.e., when tractor fuel cost less than twenty cents per gallon and before D8's sold for $200,000, "the more successful conversion projects just about break even from a benefit-cost standpoint." Alternatively, we can make more realistic assumptions regarding benefits and cost and conclude that much of the effort is a dead weight social loss.

## Divestiture as Reform for the BLM

It is obvious that there is a potential for substantial public benefits from reforms of the BLM. A review of productive range land management indicates that:

1) The BLM bureaucrats have incentives to invest our tax dollars in projects that yield negative financial returns.

2) There are high environment costs associated with two of the most ambitious BLM practices.

In general these problems result from the ambitions of well intentioned and competent administrators. Resource use is significantly determined by the incentives faced by resource managers. Public managers are no different from private in that they tend to respond to incentives. Both are largely self-interested. McKenzie and Tullock have perhaps the classic statement:

> Bureaucrats are not markedly different from other people. Most citizens of the U.S. are to some extent interested in helping their fellow man and in doing things in the public interest. Most citizens of the U.S., on the

---

[8]Workman, John P. and Charles R. Kienast. 1975. "Pinyon-juniper manipulations: some socio-economic considerations." *In* The pinyon-juniper ecosystem: a symposium pp. 163-176. Utah State Univ. Coll. Nat. Res. and Utah Agric. Exp. Sta., Logan, Utah.

other hand, tend to devote much more time and attention to their own personal interests. The same is true of bureaucrats.[9]

One explanation for the increased level of production investments in collectively owned and bureaucratically managed lands is based on the incentive structure faced by the bureaucratic managers.

For people in general, but for highly motivated individuals in particular, self-interest leads to the desire for an increase in discretionary control over resources. For the "selfish" individual, this desire provides the power and deference which accompany discretionary control. For the professionally oriented or "socially concerned" individual, this desire provides, in addition, the ability to make "good" things happen. For example, more forage growth is presumably "good" to a range manager. When resources are owned collectively as in a bureaucracy such as the U.S. Bureau of Land Management, a prime strategy for increased discretion is to promote growth of one's bureau.

As indicated in Chapter IV, there are reasons to believe that in most cases waste is generated from the bureau's budget being above optimum size. Most will agree that substantial forces lead in this direction. For the bureau head, civil service rank, prestige, and pay are all strongly related to the size of his bureau. Further, symbols of success in terms of office amenities are also related to the number of persons under his direction. In addition, expansion generates more possibilities for promotion. This enhances the ability to control those under his direction, since under Civil Service rules firings are nearly impossible to execute successfully. Thus to gain control over inferiors, the promise of promotions may be offered as inducements. And promotions are more common in a situation of growth.

Of perhaps equal importance for the ambitious bureaucrat is the fact that a large proportion of his budget is "locked in" from previous years. This, of course, reduces the range of discretionary expenditures. In contrast, new funds offer far more opportunities for flexibility and innovation.

This tendency toward growth can also be expected to encourage more intensive management of this resource. Unless the cut in manpower is small, or exercise of the authority leaves no *discretionary* resource claims, the reluctance to surrender territorial authority will also be encouraged. The desire to merge with any larger entity or to transfer resources to activities outside the agency's scope will also be discour-

---

[9]McKenzie, R. and G. Tullock, *The New World of Economics*. Richard D. Irwin, Inc., Homewood, Ill., 1975.

aged. Such incentives are consistent with maximum, as opposed to efficient, production of the resource.

This strong desire for growth does not depend on the presence of evil administrators or megalomaniacs. We must remember that the bureaucrat, because he is insulated from market information on the relative value of his product, suffers from the absence of an obvious and immediate reality check on what he prefers to believe. Thus, it is easy for him to harbor the illusion that his agency mission is of above average merit and thus argue that his office deserves about average budget increases. He, of course, has the help of clientele groups at budget time. Collective ownership and the lack of a pricing mechanism result in both anti-efficient incentives and distorted, or lack of, information which deal blows to even a well-meaning, intelligent bureaucrat from which recovery is difficult and rare. In sum, the bias is toward expanded activity.

The simplest proposal for reforming the management of BLM grazing lands would be to merely auction these lands to private parties. In addition to problems involving political feasibility, this proposal also has very serious equity implications for it would cause a serious wealth transfer. The advantages of this suggestion, however, are very substantial and merit careful consideration. The ideal policy would capture these benefits while avoiding the negative equity side effects.

First, among the advantages, private parties are in fact subjected to the reality checks imposed by balance sheets. Thus, they have strong incentives to use resources most productively in their continual search for efficiency. Investment decisions will normally entail a careful weighing of benefits against costs. Only the short-sighted or foolish private land holder would systematically engage in practices that diminish the productivity, and hence the value, of his land. Private land holders would surely not be expected to make substantial investments in actions that *were not* cost effective *but were* environmentally destructive. The welfare of bureaucrats may be advanced by using taxes for subsidizing such practices as chaining on BLM or Forest Service lands. In contrast a private rancher who receives no such subsidy, and hence must confront the economic costs and benefits, is very unlikely to persist in such unrewarding activity. Equally, the private manager is relatively unlikely to systematically overgraze his land. Thus on private lands we should expect to find economically efficient capital and management investments, an absence of environmental destruction that does not at least entail economic returns, and relatively rapid adjustments to changing circumstances. It is not that ranchers are either more moral or smarter than bureaucrats but rather that they simply face a different set of incentives. In view of these advantages why might one be reluctant to advocate a simple auctioning off of public range lands since it seems that both economic efficiency and environmental quality would be enhanced by such a move?

This reluctance is substantially based on matters of equity. Grazing rights are available at less than market rates and were initially assigned to individual ranch owners. These individuals received a windfall gain. Hence, it may not seem unfair to strip them of their windfall. In general, however, these rights have been transferred to second, third or even more distant parties. At the time of the transaction the value of the subsidized permits were capitalized into the value of grazing permits associated with a base unit ranch. For example, a ranch worth $100,000 without the permits may be worth $200,000 with them. Banks recognize this value and include it in establishing the loan value of the ranch. Thus, to deprive current owners of their permits would constitute a clear deprivation of an asset that has been legally purchased. Such an act would appear to many as an inequitable and perhaps even immoral deed. Further, it is not likely to be politically feasible.

There is, however, an alternative that captures the benefits of private ownership, generates revenue for the public treasury and does not violate standards of equity. This proposal is conceptually simple. First, separate the grazing from the other values such as mineral and wildlife. Second, calculate the discounted present value of the permit. One would calculate the present value of the income stream to the federal treasury that would be produced by the permit. Data for this computation is either currently available or can be established by a simple decision involving the determination of future fees. Third, allow present permittees to purchase property rights *in the grazing resource* at the above figure. If the present permittees do not want to exercise their option, then these rights can be put up for auction.

In sum, we suggest the sale of BLM lands with protective convenants. If rights to a tract of land are thought of as a bundle of sticks, most of those sticks would be sold, but not all. In an area providing important recreational access, for example, the land might be sold *without* the right to exclude properly behaving hikers. The right to kill certain ecologically important predators might also be withheld from sale.

Would those people currently enjoying BLM leases be disadvantaged? We think not, if the sale terms are properly established. In general, current lease holders would be offered permanent property rights to do what they are now doing plus all other land rights not specifically retained by the federal government. Making these property rights permanent would increase the value of land use to the user, since the benefits of long term management practices, such as range improvement, would clearly be captured by the user into the future. Users with a short time horizon might well choose to sell their new asset, but they would still have the incentive to avoid overgrazing, erosion, or any ohter practice which would reduce the value of their land. By the same token, such expensive (and sometimes very destructive) practices as chaining and rest-rotation grazing would be carried out only when the long-term plus short-term benefits outweighed the long-term plus short-term costs. This would be true because the land owner would both pay the costs and receive all the benefits.

The terms of sale under our divestiture plan would make available to current users the land they now utilize in return for a payment equal to the present value of all future lease payments, discounted at the rate of interest on long-term agricultural loans being made in their area. Parcels of land not bought on those terms by current lease holders would be offered at auction with a starting price equal to that offered to the current lease holder.

Diversity of land use on lands thus conveyed into the private sector would be guaranteed, for the same reason that diversity exists in an urban area: any entrepreneur with a vision of appropriate land use can bid for the right to implement his vision. Adaptiveness to changing conditions is fostered for the same reason. Those wishing to try new ideas can do so without having to convince either a giant bureaucracy or a majority of elected representatives. Ideas that turn out to be crackpot schemes are quickly exposed and stopped automatically due to the drain on the wealth of entrepreneurs and financiers. In a private setting we need not count on the goodwill or morality of decision makers; their greed will suffice. Decision makers who move the resources into higher valued uses will prosper while those who devote resources to uses others do not value highly will be sytematically separated from wealth and thus from their ability to make socially important decisions in the future.

A crucial feature of our divestiture plan is the equity of its outcome. Current users are advantaged by having available the opportunity to gain by better long-term management of the land they are using. Citizens gain not only by increased productivity, but by being able to capture the value of their productive resource into perpetuity, at least to the same degree they are doing now without having to pay the high management costs they now bear through funding the BLM.

In summary, we believe that a plan to privatize the lands currently managed by the BLM can be arranged to the benefit of everyone with the possible exception of the bureaucracy itself. The continuing and expensive hassle of intensive lobbying by environmentalists, producer groups, and others can be avoided. The ongoing debate over environmental law as it is applied to private lands will continue, of course, but the perpetual struggle over lease rates and the appropriate land use pattern will end, as will the occasional scandals which inevitably arise when public figures and bureaucrats continuously control billions of dollars and assets without any means of being held personally accountable for their use.

A basic rule of policy analysis is that there are no cost free solutions and there are no perfect solutions. This, however, is one of those rare cases in which everyone wins—or at least everyone but the bureaucrats. But they, we are told, are motivated by concern for advancing the public interest. Their reaction to this proposal may constitute a test of their claim.

# 10

## Property Rights and Natural Resources: Applications

### Property Rights to Resources and Intergenerational Equity

Since Earth Day there has been increasing attention to the resource endowment potentially available to future generations. This is certainly a reasonable concern for if the human enterprise is expected to continue for at least several generations, the question of equity clearly has temporal as well as current spatial application. If those concerned with policy analysis are to become increasingly concerned with issues of equity, there is no obvious reason to restrict this concern to a generation's time-span. Thus, we should consider transgenerational equity. Assume for a moment that no one knows into which generation he or anyone else would be born. Once behind the veil of ignorance, our key question becomes: Which assignment of property rights will produce the greater degree of intergenerational transfer, an assignment of private rights or one with collective rights assigned to a democratic government?

It is taken by many as an article of faith that we are running out of resources despite the compelling evidence of static or declining real prices for many natural resources. Certainly a perception of resource depletion is real, regardless of the facts, and it is perceptions, *not* facts, which influence policy.

Given a belief that we are running out of natural resources it follows that one should expect future generations to be seriously disadvantaged. Those with an unfortunate later birthdate will suffer as a result of conscious consumption decisions taken by their predecessors, decisions that violate intergenerational equity.

If transgenerational equity is to be a goal, then, it becomes necessary to distribute the *value* of resources across generations. Obviously, it

Adapted from Baden and Stroup's "Property Rights and Natural Resource Management," *Literature of Liberty*.

would be inequitable to distribute the volume or mass equally, for utilization efficiency will surely change. As a simple example, an equal volume of timber produces, due to higher productivity efficiency, a higher volume and value of products now than it did forty or even ten years ago. Thus, were we to be allocated the same biomass of timber as was allocated to the previous generation we would be unfairly advantaged.

Due to increased capital accumulation, including information and human capital, we expect improvements in utilization of all resources. Under incentives that reward efficiency this outcome should occur partly due to the fact that resources become increasingly scarce. In this as in other areas, however, we expect to encounter diminishing marginal returns. The gain from moving utilization of standing biomass from thirty percent to sixty percent is likely to be easier to attain than a move from sixty percent to ninety percent utilization.

The great wealth of capital stock available today was generated by the savings and accumulation of past generations. If altruism or poorly planned self-interest, the result is the same: each generation has been endowed with a continually growing stock of productive capital with which to satisfy its consumption desires as it sees fit. The natural resource equity argument is that this enhancement of consumption options is purchased at too high a price in terms of raw materials and natural amenities. Indeed, it seems reasonable to consider a possible shift in the relative opportunities offered by capital accumulation and raw materials. It is at least possible that future generations would prefer present generations to bequeath them less additional capital and more natural resources. As the authors of the Federalist Papers understood so well, no person can be assumed the best judge of another's preferences. Hence, those in the future might want the option of developing the capital that they find most useful. Clearly, however, each generation's use of resources influences the welfare of those who follow.

It is a blunt fact that the present generation operating in a historical context establishes the rules regarding property rights with respect to resources. While there may be no logical way to apply a discount rate for the comparison of satisfactions among different generations, each generation implicitly does so.

With clear property rights the market mechanism will allocate resources efficiently provided that all parties can enter the market and that negotiations have negligible costs. But because future generations cannot bargain directly with the present, this approach is questioned.

Both the issues and the conditions should now be clear. Many consider equity to be increasingly important. Transgenerational equity (discounted by the probability of their being future generations) is one important form of equity. Property rights to resources are a component in an equity formulation. And finally, future generations cannot speak for themselves.

## Property Rights and Transgenerational Equity: The Case of Exhaustible Resources

We would all expect that a market system involving privately held rights would yield very different results than would a system whose rights were held by society and decisions regarding resource use were made collectively. And it is widely believed that a market setting causes future generations to be robbed of natural resources. John Krutilla and Talbott Page, for example, recently put it this way:

> ...Generally, markets are considered fair only if all those affected by the outcomes are present in the market (without externalities) and the distribution of market power is considered fair. In the case of deciding which new (energy) supplies to develop, the distribution of market power is indeed uneven: the present generation controls the total stock of resources, leaving future generations with no voice in today's decision.[1]

If this argument were carried to its limits, the claim would be that future generations cannot bribe those in the present to forego the mildest satisfactions, even when the very survival of mankind is at issue.[2]

The major implication of this and similar material is that a market mechanism, as compared with collective control, results in future generations being deprived of resources. But this claim does not withstand examination. The explanation results from both the different incentives faced by decision makers in the two situations and from the different ways decision makers are chosen in the two settings.

In what follows, simple models of market and collective democratic actions are employed. For concreteness, the resources stock in question will be referred to as a copper mine. This example is chosen to capture the elements of inter-temporal resource allocation and intergenerational transfer of resources, while presumably minimizing the intrusion of

---

[1] John Krutilla and Talbot Page, "Paying Tomorrow for Energy Today," *Resources*, No. 49 (June 1975).
[2] For a discussion of a related issue, see: Garrett Hardin, "An Ecolate View of the Human Predicament" in Clair M. McRostie (ed.), *Global Resources: Perspectives and Alternatives* (Baltimore: University Park Press, 1980).

side issues such as environmental externalities and violation of the exclusion principle. A binary decision must be made periodically on whether to exploit the one ore body in the current period or not. Following the initial analysis, the models will be made less naive by relaxation of certain assumptions, and the resulting impacts will be noted.

To decide whether or not an existing resource should be exploited in the current time period the decision maker simply compares its value (net of development costs) in current exploitation with its expected value in highest future use (net of development costs, and discounted to the present). If current exploitation yields more net benefits, as judged by the decision makers, than does any future use, then the decision maker chooses current exploitation rather than preservation of the stock resource. The major difficulty, of course, lies in the estimation of the value in future use. The value of a body of copper ore to be mined in any given future period depends on several factors, all of which are subject to uncertainty. Availability of other copper ore, the price of copper substitutes, and technology determining copper's usefulness are all important in determining a decision maker's estimate of the mine's present value in future exploitation. For a given mine, different people are likely to have differing opinions on when the mine should be developed or, more specifically for present purposes, whether or not current exploitation is best.

The views of the populace on the present discounted value of future use might be summarized in a diagram such as the one below. The abscissa indicates E(PV), the estimated present value of preservation, which is a single value in dollar terms, expressing the summation of the influences listed above. The ordinate indicates the frequency of each estimate. No particular shape is required of the distribution for simple models. If we then locate on the abscissa a value, M, equal to the value (net of operating costs) of the ore body if mined now,[3] all E(PV) greater than the value can be characterized as indicating that preservation is preferred. Similarly, those whose E(PV) falls short of M, the current development value, presumably must conclude that current development is the better choice.

Consider now the most straightforward kind of democratic decision making regarding the copper mine. Each person expresses his opinion

---

[3]In reality, the value of the mine in "current" development is subject to some uncertainty, particularly since development is not really confined to one short time period. But the degree of uncertainty is small relative to development farther into the future. One could work with a similar, though much-compressed, distribution of estimates of value in current use, but that would seem to add complexity with no change in the basic outcome in comparing private and collective management systems.

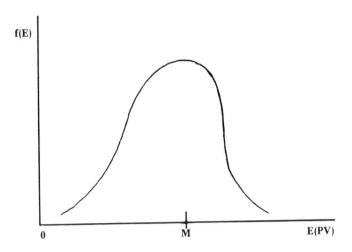

f(E)

0     M     E(PV)

of whether the mine should or should not be developed currently, and the majority rules. For a maximum bias *against* our outcome, assume that each individual is not simply self-interested, but that he votes for what he believes will benefit society most. To predict the outcome of such a vote, we simply must ask whether the majority of the estimates fall to the right, or to the left, of the value of the mine in current use. If the majority is to the left, current exploitation will be mandated; if to the right, preservation is supported. Put another way, if the median voter[4] has E(PV) greater than M, the current development value, preservation will result, while current development wins if the voter feels the other way. In a very real sense, the median voter's judgement prevails.

Alternatively, consider a simple market situation involving the same people with the same tastes, expectations, and discount rates, where the copper mine is controlled by the highest bidder. One type of bid is M, for current development, made on behalf of ore processors. The highest such bid represents the mine's worth in current exploitation. The other type of bid is from those who want to preserve the mine for the future. We can assume either altruistic or selfish motives for these bidders. In either case, each bid reflects the bidder's belief as to the mine's value. Obviously, if anyone (with sufficient funds, credit, or the ability to convince con-venturers) believes the mine will be sufficiently more valuable in future use than now, the resource will be preserved. The median opinion does not control. The tendency instead is for those *with the strongest preservation bias* to control. They are usually called speculators.

---

[4]Median voter is the individual whose E(P) splits the distribution, in the sense that half the other people lie above him, and half below.

87

We have long been puzzled regarding the general condemnation of speculators by environmentalists and preservationists. Speculator is, quite widely, a derisive term. With the singular exception of the monopoly case, such criticism seems to be at variance with the announced preferences of the critics. The critics whom we address claim to favor deferred consumption, which is merely saving for the future. This, of course, is exactly the function of the speculator. Only by paying a higher price than those who prefer to consume now can he conserve the resource for his profit (and for the future). While current consumers have good reason to object to speculators for driving up the price and hence reducing current consumption, those in the future should shower them with praise and rewards—if the speculator guessed correctly. The central point, of course, is that successful speculators benefit consumers in the future at the expense of those in the present. Their action in markets over time is analogous to distributors of goods over space. The distributor of oranges buys in Florida on behalf of New Yorkers. Florida orange prices would be lower if interstate trade were forbidden.

Whether the speculators are able to view the future period when the resource will be developed, or possess a more short-sighted view, for their own personal financial plans, is unimportant. So long as they can transfer (sell) the property rights they hold on the mine, and so long as at least a few others hold a similar view of the mine's future value, the mine remains a saleable asset and a good investment. As time passes and the higher-valued time of use approaches, the present discounted value rises.

Of course if the purchasing speculator is wrong, and potential bidders begin to discover this, he suffers the loss as the mine's value rises less rapidly (or falls) compared to other assets he could have held. He *and* the deprived earlier generation bear society's loss if his decision to preserve the mine is incorrect. *But the resource is preserved.* Since this type of speculative activity can be expected whenever resource property rights are private and transferable, resource prices in such markets will reflect bidding for future use, and *current exploitation will occur only when all speculative bids are overcome.* Contrary to the statements by Krutilla and Page, the equilibrium market price clearly includes pressure from future potential bidders, including those bidders yet unborn, since speculative bids are based on what *future* users, as bidders, are expected to be willing to pay. Hence, in a market system with transferable property rights over stock resources, those who are *most optimistic* reagrding the *future* value of any storable resource are the ones who control the resource. Given that they believe that the future value will be high, they expect to capture rewards by keeping resources out of consumption.

It is difficult to imagine how a mechanism could be devised to give current voters an analogous incentive to consider future citizens. Future voters must depend on the good will of present voters to sacrifice current consumption of governmentally controlled resources. Our analysis of collective control has thus far assumed that such good will is present: that present voters view future generations' consumption as they do their own. Previously, the only discount factor assumed to apply to consumption in the distant future was that which people apply to their own consumption during their lifetimes. This form of altruism was not required of the private bidders.

If we allow more self-interested voters to enter our collective control model, the preservation bias of the market stands out in even sharper relief. If voters are less interested in future generations' welfare than in their own, current exploitation becomes more valuable relative to the benefits of preservation in the eyes of current voters. The value in current use, M, remains constant while their effective E(PV) falls because future usefulness, enjoyed by others, is in effect more heavily discounted than if current voters themselves could enjoy the benefits.

It should be clear that, as we allow for self-interested behavior, the most realistic presumption is not what voters feel towards future generations but how they feel towards their heirs. It can be argued (particularly well in sociobiological terms) that such a presumption collapses back to the naive altruistic view. People in general may value their descendant's consumption as they do their own. However, the voters deciding on the stock of natural resources to bequeath to the next generation are not considering the welfare of their descendants alone, but the welfare of all those alive in the future. Such a diffused interest will surely result in a lower present value than that which leads people individually to leave bequests to their heirs. On the other hand, since costs are also diffuse, the net effect is not obvious.

Another assumption to be relaxed is that of market structure in the private control model. Initially we posited a competitive bidding process for the resource. In fact, a competitive market is not necessary for our results. In a monopolized or cartelized market, the tendency towards preservation is increased. As Harold Hotelling[5] demonstrated in 1931, a constant-cost monopoly will restrict the exploitation rate due to its output-restricting behavior.

---

[5]Harold Hotelling, "The Economics of Exhaustible Resources."

To summarize the situation with exhaustible resources, privately held exchangeable property rights tend to *encourage* preservation, relative to a simple democratically controlled collective management system. The gains from preservation are appropriate in a market system, but not with collective ownership, since those with expectations of high future value for the resource tend systematically to control through outbidding others. The preservation bias differential is increased if people are viewed as self-interested, or if the private producing industry is a monopoly or a cartel.

An implication of this model is at variance with commonly accepted wisdom. One respected source of that wisdom is Robert Solow who, in his 1973 Richard T. Ely lecture, stated:

> ...We know in general that even well-functioning competitive markets may fail to allocate resources properly over time. The reason, I have suggested, is because, in the nature of the case, the future brings no endowment of its own to whatever markets actually exist.[6]

We have argued that, at least relative to collective control, the future does have a representative in present markets in the form of the speculator. The endowment the future brings to the market is what the speculator expects the future to be willing to pay.

Later in the lecture Solow suggested a partial corrective to the perceived lack of representation of the future.[7] Futures markets are claimed to save resources for future generations. Our analysis suggests the opposite. To institute a futures market is to allow speculators to be supplied with both actual claims on resources and speculative claims. Without futures contracts, the speculator can only bet on the rises in resource values. Futures contracts allow speculators to sell short those resources they expect to decline in value, thereby depressing current prices and encouraging greater current consumption of those resources. In short, the futures market influences the resource market to expect a lower rise in resource price or have a higher discount rate.

Our analysis strongly indicates that a system of private property rights is consistent with preserving resources for future generations. Krutilla and Solow have correctly identified a case of market failure. Their prediction of direction, while intuitively satisfying to those opposed to the market as a resource allocating institution, appears to be exactly wrong. If this is a case of "market failure," then the failure is

[6]Robert Solow, "The Economics of Resources or the Resources of Economics," *American Economic Review* 64 (May 1974):10.
[7]*Ibid.*, p. 13.

that of saving *too much* for the future to the detriment of the present generation. From the perspective of an environmentalist-conservationist, it would be useful to analyze the mechanisms employed by the government to hasten the exploitation of resources. The implications of "do-diligence" clauses (which mandate the immediate mining of mineral and energy stocks), depletion allowances which reward early exploitation, and other tax treatments do not auger well for the natural resource endowment of the future. If the unborn could vote on the issue, to whom would they give control of resources?

## BIBLIOGRAPHY

Alchian, Armen and Allen, William. *University Economics* (3rd Edition). Belmont, California: Wadsworth, 1972.

Anonymous. Detailed Fact Sheet: *The President's Energy Program*. The White House, 1979.

Allen, Durward L. *Our Wildlife Legacy*. New York: Funk & Wagnalls, 1962.

Baden, John and Stroup, Richard. "The Environmental Costs of Government Action." *Policy Review* 4: 23–36.

Bator, Francis M. "The Anatomy of Market Failure." *The Quarterly Journal of Economics* (August 1958): 351–379.

Battelle Memorial Institute. *An Analysis of Federal Incentives Used to Stimulate Energy Production*. U.S. Department of Energy, Contract EY-76-C-06-1830 (December (1978).

Bell, Daniel. *Cultural Contradictions of Capitalism*. New York: Basic Books, 1976.

Borcherding, Thomas. *Budgets and Bureaucrats*. Durham, North Carolina: Duke University Press, 1977.

Buchanan, James. "The Case Theorem and the Theory of the State." *Natural Resources Journal* 13: (1973).

Buchanan, James and Tullock, Gordon. *The Calculus of Consent*. Ann Arbor: University of Michigan Press, 1962.

Butti, K. and Perlin, J. "Solar Water Heaters in California." *The CoEvolution Quarterly* (1977): 189–193.

Clancy, Edward P. *The Tides*. Garden City, New York: Doubleday, 1968.

Clark, Wilson. *Energy for Survival*. Garden City: Anchor Press, 1974.

Coase, Ronald. "The Problem of Social Cost." *The Journal of Law and Economics* 4 (October 1960): 1–44.

Commoner, Barry. "Interview." *Challenge* (September/October, 1979).

Coyle, D. *Electric Power on the Farm*. Washington, D.C.: United States Government Printing Office, 1936.

Culver, F. "Performance of Two Successful Windmill Generating Plants." *Electrical World* 69 (February 1917): 367–9.

Daniels, A. M. "Power For the Farm From Small Streams." *U.S. Department of Agricultural Farmers Bulletin* 1430 (1925): 1–36.

Daniels, F. *Direct Use of the Sun's Energy*. New Haven and London: Yale University Press, 1964.

Daniels, F. and Duffie, J. *Solar Energy Research*. Madison: The University of Wisconsin Press, 1955.

Deloria, Vine. *We Talk, You Listen*. New York: MacMillan Co., 1970.

Demsetz, Harold. "Toward a Theory of Property Rights." *American Economic Review* 57 (May 1967): 347–359.

Dorfman, Robert. "The Technical Basis for Decision Making." In *The Governance of Common Property Resources*. Edited by Edwin T. Haefele. Baltimore: The Johns Hopkins University Press, 1974.

Downs, Anthony. *An Economic Theory of Democracy*. New York: Harper, 1957.

Downs, James F. *The Two Worlds of the Washo: An Indian Tribe of California and Nevada.* New York: Holt, Rinehart and Winston, 1966.

Drucker, Phillip. *Cultures of the North Pacific Coast.* San Francisco: Chandler Publishing Co., 1965.

Evelyn, John. "Fumifugium: or The Inconvenience of the Aer and Smoake of London Dissipated" (written 1661). Reprinted London: National Society for Clean Air, 1961.

Farb, Peter. *Man's Rise to Civilization as Shown by the Indians of North America From Primeval Times to the Coming of the Industrial State.* New York: Dutton and Co., 1968.

Frederick, K. "Can We Put the Sun to Work?" *Scientific American* 115 (October 7, 1916): 329.

Furubotn, Eirik, and Pejovich, Svetozar. "Property Rights and Economic Theory: A Survey of Recent Literature." In *Journal of Economic Literature,* 10 (1972): 1137-1162.

Gary, T. J. and Gashus, O. K. *Tidal Power,* New York: Planum Press, 1972.

Golding, E. W. *The Generation of Electricity by Wind Power.* New York: Philosophical Library, 1955.

Gwartney, James and Stroup, Richard. *Economics: Private and Public Choice* (2nd. Edition). New York: Academic Press, 1980.

Haines, Francis. *The Buffalo.* New York: Thomas Y. Crowell Co., 1970.

Halacy, D. S. *The Coming Age of Solar Energy.* New York: Harper & Row, 1963.

Hardin, Garret. "The Tragedy of the Commons." *Science* 162 (1968): 1243-1248. Reprinted in *Managing the Commons.* Edited by Hardin and Baden.

Hardin, Garrett and Baden, John. *Managing the Commons.* San Francisco: W. H. Freeman and Company, 1977.

Heizer, R. F. "Primitive Man as an Ecologic Factor." *Kroeber Anthropological Society Papers* 15. University of California Press, 1955.

Heyne, Paul. *The Economic Way of Thinking* (2nd Edition). Chicago: SRA, Inc., 1976.

Hirsch, Fred. *Social Limits to Growth.* Cambridge: Harvard University Press, 1976.

Howe, Charles W. *Natural Resource Economics: Issues, Analysis, and Policy.* New York: John Wiley and Sons, 1979.

Ingalls, A. "Power from the Wind." *The Scientific American Digest* 134 (February 1926): 114-115.

Joskow, P. L. and Pindyck, R. S. "Those Subsidized Energy Schemes," *The Wall Street Journal* (July 2, 1979).

Kirzner, Israel. *Competition and Entrepreneurship.* Chicago: University of Chicago Press, 1973.

Krueger, Anne O. "The Political Economy of the Rent Seeking Society." *American Economic Review* 64 (June 1974): 291-303.

Landsberg, Hans; Fischman, Leonard; and Fisher, Joseph. *Resources in America's Future.* Baltimore: Johns Hopkins Press, 1963.

Leacock, Eleanor. "The Montagnais 'Hunting Territory' and the Fur Trade." *American Anthropologist* Vol. 56, No. 5, Part 2, Memoir No. 78 (1954).

Leopold, Aldo. *A Sand County Almanac and Sketches from Here and There.* New York: Oxford University Press, 1949.

Martin, Paul S. "Pleistocene Overkill." *Natural History* (December 1967).

McKean, Roland. "Products Liability: Implications of Some Changing Property Rights." *Quarterly Journal of Economics* 84 (November 1970): 611-626.

Mitchell, Edward. *U.S. Energy Policy: A Primer.* Washington: American Enterprise Institute, 1974.

Murphy, Earl F. *Governing Nature.* Chicago: Quadrangle Press, 1967.

*The Nation's Renewable Resources—An Assessment, 1975.* Washington: United States Department of Agriculture, Forest Report No. 21, June 1977.

Nisbet, Robert A. *Twilight of Authority.* New York: Oxford University Press, 1975.

Niskanen, William A., Jr. *Bureaucracy and Representative Government.* Chicago: Aldine-Atherton, 1971.

Nordhaus. "Allocation of Energy." p. 544, M.I.T. Energy Laboratory Policy Study Group, *Energy Self Sufficiency.* Washington, D.C.: American Enterprise Institute, 1974.

North, Douglass. "A Framework for Analyzing the State in Economic History." *Explorations in Economic History* 16 (1979): 249-259.

Olson, Mancur Jr. *The Logic of Collective Action*. New York: Schocken Books, 1965.

Pancratz, F. "Wind Power for Farm Electric Plants." *Mechanical Engineering* 46 (November 1924): 675-80.

Pejovich, Svetozar. *Fundamentals of Economics: A Property Rights Approach*. Dallas: The Fisher Institute, 1979.

Peltzman, Sam. "Toward a More General Theory of Regulation." *The Journal of Law and Economics* 11 (1976): 211-240.

Putman, P. *Power from the Wind*. New York: D. Van Norstrand Company, Inc., 1948.

Randall, Alan. "Property Rights and Microeconomics." *Natural Resource Journal* 15 (1975): 729-747.

Replogle, M. A. "Hydraulic Power Plant on Henry Ford Farms." *Power* 43, No. 1, (January 4, 1916).

Richman, S. "Synthetic Fuels: Economics and Politics." *Issues Analysis* (August 1979).

Ruff, Larry E. "The Common Economic Sense of Pollution." *The Public Interest* 19 (Spring 1970): 69-85.

Samuelson, Paul. "The Pure Theory of Public Expenditures." *Review of Economics and Statistics* 36 (1954): 387-389.

Saunder, R. "Harnessing the Power of Water." *Energy Primer* California: Fricke-Parks Press (1974): 148-153.

Schurr, S. H. and Netschart, B. C. *Energy in the American Economy 1850-1975*. Baltimore, Maryland: The Johns Hopkins Press, 1960.

Sencenbaugh, J. "Wind Driven Generators." *Energy Primer*. California: Fricke-Parks Press, 1974.

Shuman, F. "Feasibility of Utilizing Power from the Sun." *Scientific American* 110 (February 1914): 179.

Slattery, H. *Rural America Lights Up*. Washington, D.C.: National Home Library Foundation, 1940.

Smith, Vernon L. "The Primitive Hunter Culture." *Journal of Political Economy* 83 (August 1975): 727-756.

Speck, Frank G. "A Report on Tribal Boundaries and Hunting Areas of the Malecite Indians of New Brunswick." *American Anthropologist* 48 (1946).

_____ "Land Ownership Among Hunting Peoples in Primitive America and the World's Marginal Areas." *Twenty-Second International Congress of Americanists* 2.

Stigler, George. "The Theory of Economic Regulation" *Bell Journal of Economics and Management Science* Z (1971): 3-21.

Tuan, Yi-Fu. "Our Treatment of the Environment in Ideal and Actuality." *American Science* 58 (1970): 244-249.

Tullock, Gordon. "The Welfare Costs of Tariffs, Monopolies, and Theft." *Western Economic Journal* 5 (June 1967): 224-232.

_____ "The Cost of Transfers." *Kyklos* 24 (1971): 629-643.

von Mises, Ludwig. *Human Action*. New Haven: Yale University Press, 1949.

Weidenbaum, M. L. and Harnish, R. *Government Credit Subsidies for Energy Development*. Washington, D.C.: American Enterprise Institute for Public Policy Research, 1976.

White, Lynn Jr. "The Historical Roots of Our Ecologic Crisis." *Science* 155 (1967): 1203-1207.

Wolff, A. *The Windmill as a Prime Mover*. New York: John Wiley & Sons, 1894.

Yandle, Bruce. "The Emerging Market for Air Pollution Rights." *Regulation* (July/August 1978): 21-29.

93

11

# The Federal Budget as a Common Pool Resource: the Development of a Predatory Bureaucracy

A compelling conclusion of this volume is that there are reasons to expect a natural coalition to be emerging.[1] While the coyote may not lie down with the lamb—except for dinner—the Sierra Club member shares substantial ground with the classical liberal, the libertarian, and indeed with the fiscal conservative. In sum, environmental activists, individuals who place a high value on freedom, and those supporting reductions in the size and scope of government share substantial common interests. For quite diverse reasons, they agree that the bureaucratic entrepreneurs responsible for natural resource management systematically advocate programs that: 1) have environmental costs that exceed environmental benefits, 2) are financially irrational, and 3) increase the command sector of the economy at the expense of voluntary exchange conducted on the basis of willing consent. Although there is a surplus of examples, a brief overview of selected cases is presented below. This is followed by a presentation of the logic which produces the observed outcome. Finally, we advance a suggestion for institutional reform. The adoption of this reform would be a significant tribute to Earth Day.

## Natural Resource Mismanagement

When evaluating natural resource management by the public sector we should separate our hopes for socially optimal management from our expectations. Clearly, the natural potential and endowment of the United States is extremely favorable. In terms of strict social optimality, disregarding the distributional outcome, efficient management of this endowment dictates that inputs should be applied where marginal

Adapted from "Natural Resources and Bureaucratic Predators," John Baden and Rodney D. Fort, *Policy Review.* Winter 1980, pp. 69-81.
[1]For an overview of this process see Baden, J. and Stroup, R. "The Environmental Costs of Government Action," *Policy Review.* Spring 1978, pp. 23-38.

95

returns are highest. Further, the personnel of our land and resource management agencies tend to be both competent and well-intentioned. Yet, as indicated throughout this volume there are many examples of perverse institutional structures that systematically produce suboptimal results. Several are apparent in the important area of timber production and range land management discussed in Chapters III, IV, V, VI and IX. The essential points are briefly summarized below.

Timber production administered by the U.S. Forest Service on the National Forest system provides multiple examples of bureaucratic waste. Although the U.S. has some of the very best timber producing lands in the world, not all of this land has equal potential. The differential should be taken into account when management decisions are made. Again, management inputs should be applied where the marginal returns are highest. For example, the Northwest and the Southeast tend to have climates and soils favorable for timber production while the Rocky Mountain region is at a comparative disadvantage in timber growth potential. Although trees will grow in the Rockies, the inputs are higher per unit of output than in the Northwest or Southeast. Much of this land is perhaps most valuable for its recreational, grazing, and mining potential.

While those familiar with forestry recognize these facts, decisions regarding public timber management are largely based on political considerations. Thus, Forest Service representatives from *every* region advocate enhanced funding for timber management in *their* region *regardless* of different potentials among regions. Ideally, efforts directed toward timber production would be guided by consideration of marginal net benefits. In the private sector the incentives are such that this happens. In contrast, the public sector shows less sensitivity to marginal costs and benefits.

The Forest Service appraises timber and if the appraisal value exceeds a minimum base price, the timber is auctioned to the highest bidder. Usually—but not always—the short-term costs of administration are met. The appraised price set by the Forest Service *does not,* however, take into account long-run costs over the timber growing cycle. As a result, a substantial portion of public timber is harvested at a net social loss *in spite of the fact that much of the existing inventory was grown at a zero cost.*

Obviously, a private firm that followed this pattern would get out of business or go bankrupt. In effect, the Forest Service utilizes the "profits" from productive sites to balance the losses incurred by inefficient and environmentally harmful logging on unproductive timber land.

Additional losses are made up from federal taxes. Although the process is economically inefficient and environmentally destructive, it is supported by agency personnel and by those in the local economy who benefit from the subsidies.

## The Trials of Range Land Management

The Bureau of Land Management in the U.S. Department of the Interior administers 171 million acres of public land in eleven western states (This area is larger than the combined acreage of Wyoming, Utah and Idaho). This land is arid and predominantly used for grazing. It is no accident that it is also the hotbed of the "Sage Brush Rebellion."

Until 1964 the primary job of the BLM was to administer grazing privileges on public lands. Under the Federal Land Policy and Management Act of 1976, the BLM is required to manage in accord with the principles of multiple use and sustained yield.

Because of overstocking caused by the common pool attributes of the range land, deterioration and erosion became severe. By the 1930's ranchers recognized that investments in institutional reform would be productive.[2] Thus, in June of 1932 the Taylor Grazing Act established the Grazing Service in the Department of Interior. As a result of general dissatisfaction with management, the Grazing Service and the General Land Office were consolidated into the Bureau of Land Management in 1946. Unfortunately, reorganization did not solve the problems.

The agency acknowledges that the lands under its jurisdiction are *not* properly managed, that conditions are actually declining in many areas, and that those conditions are expected to decline further under the present system. These admissions of failure prompt the agency to request increased funding. A substantial portion of the additional funding is directed toward a "new" management system called "rest rotation grazing." (discussed in Chapter IV)

---

[2]For a delightful treatment of institutional innovations by ranchers see Terry Anderson and P. J. Hill, "From Free Grass to Fences: Transforming the Commons of the American West," in Hardin and Baden, *Managing the Commons*, W. H. Freeman, 1977.

B. L. M., 1975, *Range Condition Report Prepared for the Senate Committee on Appropriations*. U.S. Dept. of Interior. Washington, D.C.: U.S. Government Printing Office.

Rozell, D. G., *et al. Economic Returns of Rest Rotation Grazing to the Bureau of Land Management*. University of Nevada, Reno, 1973.

## The Logic of Bureaucratic "Irrationality"

The term "bureaucrat" has been used to identify the decison-makers in government administrative agencies. Typically, these individuals are public servants whose public actions are presumed to be in the public interest. Yet, as demonstrated throughout this volume, public resource management agencies engage in actions that are, from our strict description of social welfare, economically and environmentally "irrational." The financial and environmental benefits of many programs are swamped by the financial and environmental costs. It becomes increasingly apparent to many observers that our public servants often produce benefits that can only serve some concentrated groups and the bureaucrat who generates those benefits. Cynical condemnation of the public servants often follows this conclusion. While this may provide psychic unguent, it retards remedial action by diverting attention from the causes of perverse bureaucratic outcomes. Focus on "bad" bureaucrats clouds the issue. Bureaucrats of even the purest intentions cannot be expected to produce results consistent with the welfare of their "wards" if by so doing they harm their own professional welfare.[3] Since bureaucratic outcomes frequently violate the public interest, we contend that the incentive structures faced by bureaucrats are of a perverse nature; incentives are responsible for outcomes. The problem, we stress, is *not* one of "bad" people but rather one of faulty institutional design.

Ironically, government fails in the role of public-interest maximizer for the same reasons that markets sometimes fail. The perceived costs of individual decision-makers in government do not accurately reflect the total social costs of their decisions; government fails because perceived individual costs and true social costs of government decisions diverge. Hence, it can be expected that government output will be socially non-optimal and governmental budgets larger than optimal.

We argue that the size of government is socially non-optimal. We can further argue that government growth can be traced to two ideas: 1) that government will succeed in overcoming the problems that cause markets to fail, and 2) that investments in influencing governmental decisions may be profitable. The first belief lacks compelling corroborating evidence, yet it continues to flourish. The second, unfortunately, is in fact substantially correct under the currently existing institutional

---

[3]To request that individuals behave counter to their interests violates the Cardinal Rule of Public Policy: "Never ask a person to act against his own self-interest." See Garrett Hardin, *The Limits of Altruism* (Indiana Univ. Press, 1977) p. 27.

structure. The divergence between the costs faced by the individual decision-maker and the total social cost resulting from his decision makes government too big, and the continually increasing propensity of government decision-makers to provide concentrated benefits for special interest groups leads to government growth. The increasing ability of government to disperse the costs of these special benefits over all taxpayers (or even onto future elections and generations), fueled by the belief that government will succeed where markets fail, could perhaps be termed a "hole in the dike" which allows these increased transfers.

Terry Anderson and P. J. Hill provide substantial evidence in support of the argument that the U.S. has recently become, and continues to be, an ever-larger "transfer society."[4] As they state in their introductory chapter,

> ...the early American experience was one in which transfer activity was very limited and productive activity was encouraged. But because of the alterations in the institutional framework or the rules under which economic activity takes place, that situation has reversed. We are now a society in which transfer activity is encouraged at the expense of productive activity.[5]

Their argument hinges on the idea that the continuous altering of social rules, i.e., the courts' interpretation of the Constitution, has favored transfer-seeking activities. Since transfer activities occur in the political arena, the result of the continuous change of the rules in favor of transfer-seeking has resulted in government growth and will continue to do so as long as the rules are so altered.

An important conclusion to be drawn from the preceding logic is that more support for a bureaucratic agency can be generated by increasing benefits selectively than by reducing costs generally. It is bureaucratically profitable to cultivate a concentrated group of beneficiaries. We can not overstress the importance of understanding that government growth is the result of rational behavior. Hence, it is patterned and, thus, predictable. We can understand its cause. Favor-seeking and favor-provision are marginally beneficial! Anderson's and Hill's "transfer society" flourishes.

The above propensity of government to increase transfers has generated a growing administrative force to carry out the transfers. It is this shifted focus toward bureaucratic administration of transfers which

---

[4]Anderson, Terry L. and Hill, P. J., *The Birth of A Transfer Society*, Hoover Institution Press (in press).
[5]*Ibid.*, p. 5.

leads us to the following examination of bureaucrats and the "treasury commons." Just as early ranchers over-used the range commons, bureaucracies over-exploit the treasury commons.

## Abuse of the Treasury Commons

The elements contributing to a commons—non-exclusive ownership and self-maximizing behavior of actors—exist in government in sufficient quantity so that one may justify labeling that portion of the treasury allocated to bureaucratic budgets as a commons. Accepting the treasury as a common pool resource allows the application of Hardin's "tragedy of the commons" model.[6] Essentially, the logic as it applies to this case is identical to that of the ranchers on common grazing lands. Seeking to maximize his budgetary discretion (we agree with Niskanen[7]), each bureaucrat realizes that he has access to the treasury. He can be seen as asking the question, "What is the gain to my organization (hence, to me) of capturing another increment of the treasury?" All of the increase would go to finance his agency's activities (hence, enhancing the bureaucrat's discretionary control of resources), while the costs of his capture are spread among the entire community of bureaucrats in terms of lost capture opportunities. All bureaucrats realize that the same calculus holds for them and that it is rational for each to capture additional increments of the treasury. With each bureaucrat having an incentive to increase his capture of the treasury, he must find ways of increasing his agency's magnitude and the scope of activity. Hence, each bureaucrat has incentive to pursue programs that concentrate benefits while dispersing costs, as in the examples we mentioned. While Hardin deals with the analogy of human-ecosystem interations (his example is of herdsmen on a common pasture), human-human interactions are equivalent.

To conclude this discussion of the tragedy of the treasury commons, let us recall that it is the willingness of individuals to pay taxes that ultimately limits the treasury. It is the taxpayer's income that, unwittingly or not, actually falls prey to the institutional treasury commons. Losses inherent in the "tragedy of the treasury commons" are borne by all society members in the form of lost control over productive resources and a relaxation of the "rule of willing consent." The more decisions

[6]Hardin, Garrett, "The Tragedy of the Commons," *Science*, 162: 1243–1248, 1968.
[7]Niskanen, William A., Jr., *Bureaucracy and Representative Government* (Aldine-Atherton, 1971).

that are made over any individual's resources without his consent, the greater the chance that a decision will be unsatisfactory to that individual. This will affect each of us as the scope and magnitude of the public sector increases. By most criteria, then, these losses are in a currency of ever increasing scarcity—freedom in everyday life. As Hardin so aptly states, "Freedom in the commons brings ruin to all." Pursuit of bureaucratic self-interest in the treasury commons is predicted to bring tragedy when all bureaucrats, according to their incentive structure, set such a course.

Several generations of economists and others interested in policy analysis have noted that a very substantial proportion of legislation has socially wasteful impacts. At a time when many resources are perceived as becoming more scarce, many people are disturbed by this waste. Further, most of the above economists bemoan the brute reality that their analyses are noted and then ignored - or merely ignored - in the political sector. Except for those lost in the wonder of their display of analytical creativity, the reaction is a feeling of hurt resignation. Hence, the economist applying cost benefit analysis to federal projects is a contemporary analogue of Sisyphus. Rather than roll stones endlessly up slopes never to reach the top, the analysts endlessly unroll printouts in committees, never to make their point. Hence the potential utility of their product is unrealized. Neither good intentions nor good products will suffice. Too many interests have too large an incentive to ignore the output.

Decisions are made on the basis of information and incentives. In the case we address, there is little incentive to utilize the information available. There is at least one obvious institutional solution to the problem: the creation of a "predatory bureaucracy."

The literature on bureaucratic pathology is voluminous and growing rapidly. In its traditional form it exists in Public Administration, Political Science, and Sociology. Recent advances, however, have come largely from applying economic logic to the area. The bottom line of studies from each of these areas remains fairly consistent with the following: bureaucrats operate to increase their discretionary control over resources. In sum, they operate to expand their budget.

Writing on the Civil Service Reform Act signed in October of 1978, Stephen Miller, a Resident Fellow at the American Enterprise Institute, notes that:

> Of course the new law will not solve the problem of bureaucracy. Nothing really will. Bureaucracy is less a problem than a disease of modern civili-

101

zation, one that can be treated but not cured. Like air pollution, one can't do away with it altogether.[8]

Miller continues:

Given the dynamics of the Washington establishment, it is extremely difficult to eliminate ongoing programs. In order to do so, a counter-constituency has to be organized, one that is srongly opposed to a particular program. But it is hard to organize people to oppose something unless they have compelling reasons to do so. People are against inflation, bureaucracy, unemployment, or abortion; rarely are they against a particular federal program. Once a program—or a set of programs organized under the rubric of an agency—is put into motion, it tends not only to stay in motion but also to stay on the same course, not changing its way of doing things until scandal throws it off course."[9]

## The Predatory Budget

A predator is an animal (or occasionally a plant) that captures and extracts his sustenance from other animals. Could this mode of existence be replicated and introduced in a bureaucratic environment to slow down bureaucratic growth? Conceptually the answer is yes—but objections should be anticipated. First, what is the structure?

Assume that an agency, The Bureau of Budgetary Control (BBC), is initiated as a one-sided agency. Similar to the E.P.A., it is admittedly designed to represent *one* position and serve as an advocate of one fundamental goal. Like the EPA, whose primary mission is to advocate protection of the environment at whatever cost, the Bureau of Budgetary Control would advocate budgetary reductions. The design problems become (1) providing incentives to perform and (2) structuring incentives for this bureau to prey upon those budgetary items whose social costs promise to swamp the social benefits.

Further, assume that this agency is established with a one-time appropriation that will carry it for two years only. This constraint is critical. It is at this point that we harness the fundamental pathology of bureaucracies: that propensity toward perpetuation and growth for social benefit. Continual funding, and hence survival and growth, are dependent upon predation of other agencies' budgetary requests. We quoted above Miller's statement: "But it is hard to organize people to oppose something unless they have compelling reasons to do so." This

---

[8]Miller, Stephen A., "A Good Word for Bureaucracy," *American Spectator*, 12 (Feb. 1979): 14–17.
[9]*Ibid.*

strategy provides compelling opportunities for the proposed Bureau of Budgetary Control.

Assume, for example, that the Bureau of Reclamation requests $250 million to rebuild Teton Dam, again primarily as a flood control project. A number of local farmers who grow subsidized grain and sugar beets support this project. It is obvious that this particular project is of extremely dubious value on net. Hence, the Bureau of Budgetary Control would marshall evidence against the project in direct opposition to the testimony developed by the Bureau of Reclamation and its clientele groups. In this case they would join with the Wilderness Society, Friends of the Earth, and so forth.

If the proposal for funding the rebuilding of Teton Dam is rejected by Congress, two budgetary transfers are made. First, the BBC receives one percent of the requested budgetary item. Second, the proposing agency, in this case the Bureau of Reclamation, suffers a budget cut of one percent of the project's proposed operating costs from its operating budget. (These figures are strictly arbitrary and are likely to benefit from adjustment based on experience.)

The major advantage of this proposed system is that it counters the problem of legislation that concentrates benefits while diffusing costs. Further, it builds into the appropriation process a spokesman for the public interest—more importantly, a spokesman who does good while doing well. In sum, by employing this system we rely upon self-interest to advance the public interest. There are, of course, a few technical problems with this proposal, but they are likely to be minor when compared with the benefits.

One likely objection is fundamentally visceral: the charge that we are creating another bureaucracy. Such a creation, presumably is bad *a priori*—and the objection is understandable. It will not, however, stand up to analysis. A bureau is merely a tool of social organization. As such it must be evaluated in terms of its output rather than its mere existence. Clearly the incentive structures in bureaucracies often lead to socially costly outcomes associated with goal displacement, growth past the point where marginal social costs equal marginal social benefits, and a host of other pathologies. In this case, however, we harness this incentive structure to counter common bureaucratic pathologies. Analogies to this situation are common in the area of medical biochemistry.

The second objection is that the BBC may kill some worthwhile programs. Indeed it might. All drugs, especially the most useful, do as a matter of fact kill some patients. So do seat belts. Is the agency, however, beneficial on net? Clearly such an agency as the BBC would select as prey the programs that are the most vulnerable to attack: those whose social payoffs are demonstrably highly negative. The size of the BBC is, to put it crudely, a function of the stupidity of the prey agencies. A series of successful attacks is very likely to have a profound effect upon the learning curve of the various agencies. At first, successful attacks are likely to generate doubts regarding the worth of other programs. Since the agencies are uncertain regarding which of their programs may be subject to predation, they will have strong incentives to avoid proposing projects of dubious social utility. Should this be the case, policy is likely to be more carefully analyzed. The implications for the economics profession are obvious.

When writing in this area it is increasingly difficult to end cheerfully. Our proposal is merely the first cut on a difficult problem. We realize that it stands in need of refinement. While our proposal may seem radical when first considered, it will seem less so if reconsidered. In view of the direction the United States has been heading, there will be increasing incentives to reconsider. Given the avowedly experimental character of our political institutions, some proposal similar to ours is likely to capture the attention of at least one political entrepreneur. It is, in the final analysis, difficult to constrain a fundamental optimism regarding the ability of people to learn when self-interest is at stake. Such learning is likely to have beneficial impacts for the environment, the economy, and in particular for the voluntary sector of the economy.

# 12

## Concluding Thoughts on
## Earth Day Reconsidered

With our tradition of pragmatic activism, we Americans are compulsive in our willingness to tackle tough social problems. Whenever we perceive a problem or an injustice, we can count on the emergency of a hero, a heroine, or a coalition to propose some way to "fix" the problem.

As predictable as these heroic responses are, they have traditionally been preoccupied with results rather than processes. Public spirited reactions to the environment, inflation, unemployment, energy and all the other issues of the day are *result*, rather than *process* oriented. If we think too many trees are being cut, we simply legislate that fewer trees be cut. If we are disturbed by inflation, we propose the adoption of price controls. If we are concerned by unemployment rates, we propose that government create additional jobs. In each case, we focus directly on the desired result rather than on the processes or mechanisms which might reasonably be expected to lead to a preferred condition.

Enter the economist as the curmudgeon with the message that good intentions are not enough to achieve desirable ends. It is the process that counts. Processes are not only important, they are critical to producing desired results. Since the economic and political landscape is littered with the wreckage of well-intentioned but disappointing programs, the warnings of the economists cannot be ignored by the thoughtful activist. Environmental programs, some of which are evaluated in this volume, have not fulfilled their positive promises on the one hand, and have led to unanticipated negative consequences on the other. Enough evidence is now available to suggest that the resulting frustration cannot be eliminated by means of "better" programs with "better" people running them. Instead, it is obvious that more attention should be devoted to the processes that led to the original, undesirable outcome as well as to the processes set in motion when we adopt programs to "solve" the perceived problems.

M. Bruce Johnson
Johnson is Professor of Economics at the University of California, Santa Barbara.

The economist's intellectual perspective on these matters is so similar to that of the environmentalist that one wonders why a partnership between the two was not formed in the natural course of events. Environmentalists believe that the ecological system is a collection of interconnected and interdependent parts. An exogenous change in one sector or sub-system will lead to a chain reaction of effects elsewhere.

Economists hold the identical view with respect to the economic system. General equilibrium models are a formal way of saying that "everything depends on everything else." Moreover, it is axiomatic in economics that individuals make choices with some specific purpose in mind. Hence, given different opportunities, individuals will respond in different ways. Perhaps more to the point, prices and incentives *do* make a difference to the outcome. The lesson for environmental policy is simply that the programs used, however well intentioned, will fail if the incentives buried in the institutional structure are ignored or poorly designed.

What difference does this make? A great deal in both theory and practice. An environmental improvement program that neglects its effects on the incentives of interested parties will lead to unintended consequences. For example, one of the essays in this volume documents the government's practice of harvesting timber in areas where the cost of harvesting exceeds the gross monetary value of the timber sold. In this case, government action leads to a net waste of resources and, one can argue, to a degradation of the environment. How can this behavior be explained except by a perverse incentive structure for the government bureaucrats responsible? Assuming they want neither to waste resources nor to spoil the environment, their behavior must be a purposeful, reasoned response to the incentive structure in which they find themselves operating. It must be in their best interest to so act. A similar analysis could be made with respect to the practice of chaining timberland in order to create grazing land of marginal, if not negative, net value.

But the failure of environmental programs cannot be blamed wholly on the bureaucracy; various segments of the public are also systematically advantaged or disadvantaged by environmental programs and these individuals and groups naturally adjust to the new programs in order to either make the best of a bad situation, cut their losses, or beat the system. That, too, is rational behavior that an economist would trace to the incentive structure and the prices implicit in the environmental progam. Again, it is surprising that the environmentalist sponsors of a program would not anticipate the feedback and interdependence in the political and economic realm with the same degree of insight that they have in the ecological realm. This natural, purposeful behavior by affected parties—whether bureaucrats or otherwise—subverts the programs.

In a more general sense, the environmentalists also confuse normative and positive issues. To be specific, since many environmentalists believe that environmental amenities *should* be free to all, they support and promote programs intended to produce environmental amenities free of user charges. Here the economic distinction between price and cost is relevant.

The program may indeed set the *prices* of environmental goods at zero, but the true *costs* incurred by society are unambiguously positive! These costs are measured in terms of the foregone alternatives. For example, if a commercially viable forest is set aside for aesthetic purposes, the cost of the amenities thus produced can be measured in terms of higher timber prices and lower receipts, taxes and employment in the immediate vicinity. The fact that environmental amenities associated with an untouched forest are assigned a zero price (i.e., given away free) only masks the real costs of the program and deludes the public. Furthermore, when the prices of environmental goods are set at zero (or, at least, set much lower than the true costs), a certain dynamic process is set in motion. The public believes the environmental goods are free and, as a consequence, rationally demands that still more goods be produced. Why not, if it is free?

This pricing policy and the resulting dynamic are not unique to environmental programs, by any means. Government and its special interest allies will systematically underprice the output of their programs on a case-by-case basis. The systematic understatement of prices of environmental and other goods and services produced by government has far-reaching implications in an interdependent and interconnected economic system. Most people rely on prices as an efficient source of information to guide their purchases. When typical consumer buys a phonograph record in the private marketplace, he does not have to become informed about the price of the appropriate plastics, pressing equipment, delivery and packaging costs, etc. All of that information is summarized in the final price of the record. In the case of government goods, the typical consumer/taxpayer also looks to the "market" price as his source of information. If the government quotes a price lower than the true cost of the goods or services, individual consumers and the group can be expected to want more of the government output than would be the case if the higher, correct price were quoted.

This conclusion is critical. Who among the general public really knows the true costs of producing environmental goods? If the government does not assign the correct price to the output, can the individual citizen reasonably be expected to engage in laborious and intricate cost benefit analyses? Moreover, the citizen/taxpayer with a special interest axe to grind is encouraged to engage in strategic behavior: he correctly reasons that the cost of his special program will be divided among the general public and consequently his personal benefit/cost ratio will be high. This is similar to the situation in which ten people going out to dinner agree beforehand to divide the total check for the group equally, even though each individual can order whatever he or she pleases. If a dinner is a one-time affair with strangers, the rational diner will reason as follows: "If we all order a $10.00 dinner, the total check will come to $100.00 and I will pay $10.00. But, if I order a $20.00 dinner while the other nine order the $10.00 dinner, the total check will be $110.00 and we will each pay $11.00. Thus, I will get a $20.00 dinner for $11.00." Extend the logic to the next step. Since each diner has an incentive to splurge, can there be any doubt that the total amount of money spent on the dinner will be greater under the "equal share" agreement than under an arrangement where each diner paid his or her own check?

The analogy to the production of government goods financed out of the general tax fund is clear. Each special interest group will lobby to increase the activity level of its own pet projects on the rational expectation that the bulk of the costs will be passed on to the larger tax-paying public. The net result is a larger public expenditure than each citizen would freely choose in the absence of this perverse incentive structure. Adopting user charges for most, if not all, governmentally produced goods and services would internalize the costs and produce both better levels and better mixes of output. Failing that, government activity must be directed by distributional or equity considerations that are arbitrary, at best.

Perhaps more to the point, the production of "free" public goods by citizens leads to strategic gaming behavior by citizens and to the disappointments and inefficiencies so clearly documented in this volume. The axiom "There is no such thing as a free lunch" also extends to free vistas, air quality, wilderness areas, and grazing land.